P9-AFW-133

The Cocktails of The Ritz Paris

Colin Peter Field

Illustrations **Yoko Ueta**

The Cocktails of The Ritz Paris

BAR HEMINGWAY
RITZ PARIS

SIMON & SCHUSTER
New York London Toronto Sydney Singapore

A propos

I possess an extensive (one might even say exhaustive) collection of cocktail books from all over Europe and the United States, and I have spent hours learning the recipes contained within. It has often occurred to me during my studies that one of the major faults of all these otherwise fascinating tomes is that they give no real information on who, where, when or even why individual cocktails were invented. This is understandable: the origin of a cocktail can be, as we shall see, a difficult fact to establish. For example, a friend and fellow bartender who has written several books tells me that even the source of a cocktail as recent as the Cosmopolitan – a veritable world-wide classic – is almost impossible to trace!

A big problem for the cocktail genealogist is the amount of apocryphal stories put about by famous bars that claim to be the birthplace of certain cocktails. As so often happens with myths, if they get repeated often enough, they acquire factual status, even in the eyes of the people who propagated them in the first place!

Of course, not all cocktails' origins are completely obscure. We have pretty solid information on such cocktails as the Gin Fizz from London, the Ramos Fizz from New Orleans, the Singapore Sling from Raffles in Singapore, or the Jennings Cox Daiquiri (named after the mines in Cuba). Then we have the Gibson from Charles Dana Gibson at the bar of the Plaza Hotel in New York, and the Bellini from Harry Cipriani's Bar in Venice (superb, by the way, when accompanied by one of their priceless carpaccios).

We can state with confidence that most cocktails come into being to mark a celebration, be it of an event or a person. But when the cocktail itself gathers a degree of fame, it can, unfortunately, happen that people who had nothing to do with its conception hijack its discovery for themselves.

Furthermore, those who write about cocktails quite often copy other writers' work word-for-word; if the original source is wrong and it goes unchallenged, well, you can see how erroneous facts get spread around.

So, how do we establish the truth? The following example shows just how tricky that can be.

The difficulty in finding the truth about a cocktail
Bernard 'Bertin' Azimont, the bartender of the Ritz Paris's Petit Bar (and, later, Head Bartender of the hotel), told me one day over lunch how he invented the Bloody Mary in the 1950s: he had, he said, concocted it for Ernest Hemingway. The doctors had forbidden the writer to drink. Mary, Hemingway's wife, had taken the interdiction very seriously and had placed him under close watch. Stealth and cunning were needed, and so it was that Bertin devised the ingenious mixture, a drink packed full of alcohol that could not be detected on the writer's breath. Hemingway, he said, was so pleased that he had got the better of his 'bloody wife' that he named the

drink after her. And thus came to pass, one might imagine, the Bloody Mary. If only it were that easy: there exists a letter written by Hemingway himself in 1947 giving the precise recipe for the Bloody Mary, offering information that he had enjoyed it in China as early as 1941.

Perhaps Bertin invented the cocktail earlier than he remembers. Perhaps Bertin did not invent the cocktail at all. A.E Hotchner's biography *Papa Hemingway* confirms that Bertin's 'inimitable Bloody Marys' were a central part of the writer's ritual for deciding upon which horses he would place bets at this time, but, of course, that is not proof that Bertin devised the recipe.

A lot of books maintain that it was Fernand Petiot of Paris (and later of New York at the St.Regis in the 1930s) that invented it. Clearly, we have to dig a little deeper, and take more of a serious historical approach.

In the years following the 1917 Russian Revolution, vodka was very, very scarce. In fact its distillation was banned until 1936. Only beer, wine and an insipid type of vodka (no stronger than 20° abv) could be sold. All production was controlled by a national monopoly. In his *Du Monde j'ai fait le tour*,

Vladimir Maïakovski states that the favourite mixed drink of the hundreds of thousands of Russians and Polish living in the United States was actually gin and ginger ale. This was sometimes called 'American Champagne' or 'Prohibition Champagne'. In point of fact, one can already see the grains of the Moscow Mule cocktail (vodka and ginger beer) in this brew.

It would seem that a certain Vladimir Arsenyevitch was entrusted with the exploitation of the 'Smirnov' (as it was written at the time) vodka outside of Russia after the Revolution. He tried to set up distilleries in Istanbul and then in Poland, but all his efforts came to nothing. Having moved to France, he changed his name to 'Smirnoff' and created a company called Pierre Smirnoff, after Piotr Arsenyevitch who had made Smirnov Vodka's production plant Russia's largest vodka distillery. Smirnoff's first distillery was set up just outside Paris in 1928. It went bust within three months. Nice followed; same result. By 1933 certain production rights had been sold to the United States, and these eventually fell into the hands of the Heublein Company. By 1934, vodka, although not technically referenced in the United States, was legal. (And dear old Fernand Petiot was now working in the St.Regis Hotel serving, it would seem, Red Snappers, later referred to as the polite version of

the Bloody Mary.) Real improvements for vodka sales, however, would not come until just after the Second World War.

The first tomato juice cocktail, according to Frank Meier's 1936 *Cocktail Book*, was invented by the College Inn Food Product Company of Chicago, circa 1928. Salt and Worcestershire sauce are to be found in the 'cocktail', but no alcohol. Now, Chicago was also the home of the famous 'Bucket of Blood Club' for newspaper men in the 1920s, and guess who was a newspaper man in the 1920s and was born in Oak Park, Chicago in 1899? Ernest Hemingway!

When Bertin told the world in the early 1970s about his cocktail nobody seemed to dispute the claim. There seems to be no true evidence, available to me, that is, of this cocktail before the 40s. Jack Hemingway, the writer's first son from his 1921 Hadley Richardson marriage, once secretly confided to me that he didn't remember drinking the Bloody Mary until after the Second World War!

Here, however, is an extract of a letter, afore mentioned, written to Bernard Peyton by Ernest Hemingway on 5 April 1947.

'Dear Bernie,

To make a pitcher of Bloody Mary (any smaller amount is worthless) take a good sized pitcher and put in it as big a lump of ice as it will hold. (This to prevent too rapid melting and watering of our product.) Mix a pint of good Russian vodka and an equal amount of chilled tomato juice. Add a tablespoon full of Worcestershire sauce, Lea and Perrins is usual, but can use AI or any good beefsteak sauce. Stirr (with two rs). Then add a jigger of fresh squeezed lemon juice. Stirr. Then add small amounts of celery salt, cayenne pepper, black pepper. Keep on stirring and taste it to see how it is doing. If you get it too powerful, weaken with more tomato juice... I introduced this drink to Hong Kong in 1941 and believe it did more than any other single factor except perhaps the Japanese army to precipitate the fall of that Crown Colony. After you get the hang of it you can mix it so it will taste as if it [had] absolutely no alcohol of any kind in it and a glass of it will still have as much kick as a really good big Martini... There is vodka made in N.J. by a Russian process that is ok. Can't remember the name...'

Hemingway goes on to recommend, '*a fine Mexican sauce called Esta Si Pican (sort of mild Tabasco) that is good added to the Bloody Marys, too. Just a few drops*'.

One can see the challenge that faces the cocktail historian!

I'm hoping that this book will provoke a few bars to really talk to me about their cocktail heritage. If only the bartender who really did invent this cocktail had written a book at the time, nobody would be able to doubt the parentage of this cocktail today. We can all dream... I can't resist adding that George Jessel, Toastmaster General of the United States, did announce quite fervently in the Smirnoff vodka campaign circa 1955 that it was he that had invented the Bloody Mary! It takes a lot of courage and faith in oneself to stand up and be counted and nobody truly contested his claim in public.

In search of the Sidecar Cocktail

5/10 cognac

3/10 Cointreau

2/10 lemon juice

Pour the ingredients into a shaker.
Serve in a cocktail glass.

There are several bars in the world that lay claim to the invention of this cocktail. Perhaps they all sincerely believe they did. However, let me offer you this extract from one of the most sought-after cocktail books in the

world, *The Stork Club Bar Book*, written by Lucius Beebe and published in 1946:

'The Sidecar was, to the best of the knowledge and belief of the author, invented by Frank, steward and senior barkeep of the celebrated Paris Ritz Bar during the golden age of the early twenties.

'In an era when Joe Zelli's, Harry's New York Bar and the men's bar on the Cambon side of the Ritz were probably the three best known tippling Taj Mahals in the world and when every Atlantic liner set down hundreds of solvent and thirsty Yanks full of devaluated francs, Frank of the Ritz Bar was a sort of universally recognised king of saloonkeepers and was, in fact, a very pleasant, generous and understanding friend to thousands of Americans.

'There was nothing either cheap or popular about the Ritz and there was no dandruff in the morning jackets of its customers, who included Evander Berry Hall, the then King of Spain, the Prince of Wales, Phil Plant, William B. Leeds and the Russian Grand Dukes then living in exile in Paris. The men's bar was also the happy romping and stomping grounds, in summer, of most of Harvard, Yale and Princeton with an occasional democratic leaven of Williams or Dartmouth.

'The Sidecar was invented by Frank, so far as fallible human memory can determine, about 1923 as a sort of companion piece to the Stinger, only with even more expensive ingredients. It was always built by Frank for favoured customers with Ritz's own bottling of a Vintage 1865 Cognac and set one back, in this redaction (1946) the then equivalent of five American dollars'.

Everything seems to ring perfectly true in this account; even the way Mr. Beebe mentions that Frank was a 'generous and understanding friend to thousands of Americans'. When one knows the story of those 'devaluated' francs one can imagine how understanding Frank was! I say 'bravo' to Frank Meier. However, in the last years of his career, Frank actually became a victim of his own professionalism and understanding: in order for his regular clients to be able to drink normally in the Bar, Frank paid their bills for them, asking them to credit his bank account in England. Frank clearly forgot that this was an illegal exercise. Before I go on I will admit that as a Head Bartender I would have definitely done everything in my power to satisfy my own clientele. A good bartender will do anything to keep the hotel's bar going, even working 23 hours in one stint (as this author did on New Year's Eve 1999-2000).

Anyhow, back to the Sidecar. A lot of facts about Frank's ownership of the cocktail do seem to add up, but... why didn't Frank Meier 'sign' the Sidecar in his usual manner in his famous 1936 book, *The Artistry of Mixing Drinks*? John MacQueen's 1903 cocktail book has no mention of it, nor does the famous Grand Hotel Paris Head Bartender, Frank P. Newman, in his superb book *American-Bar* (1907). A certain Robert of the Embassy Club in London wrote in his 1922 book *Cocktails – How to Mix Them* that the inventor of the Sidecar was a bartender named MacGarry working at the Bucks Club. The *Savoy Cocktail Book* of 1930 mentions the Sidecar, and, five years later, *Old Mr. Boston* even gives its exact recipe… but no names are offered for its inventor.

The Cognac Ritz Paris, 'Vintage 1865'. This cognac is a reality. I've served it on many an occasion, as I have the 1812, 1830 and 1834 versions. Actually, the 1813 is the favourite of a lot of my clients, and it's my personal preference, too. I can say that I have served these exceptional cognacs to my clients so many times that a few (though only a few) actually have preferences for one 'pre-phylloxera' to another. The magic of these marvellous people is such that, while arguing a difference of opinion, they have been known to offer their favourite pre-phylloxera to their opponent in an attempt to prove a point! One such client – we'll call him Noah – on hearing one evening that two people in the Bar were celebrating a special wedding anniversary, offered the elderly couple in question (who were not quite at ease in the Bar, but had visibly waited a long time to come to the Ritz Paris for an unforgettable cocktail) two of the 1850s.

As I write these lines, a bottle of Vintage 1830, Ritz Paris aged and guaranteed fine Champagne Cognac is on sale to only a few of our special customers at 100,000 French francs (or 14,815 Euros) We do not have an endless stock of this very special product, so I'm sure the reader will understand our reluctance to separate ourselves from part of the Ritz Paris heritage.

This is all part of cocktail detective work and it's a passionate hobby. Some bartenders would rather maintain the lore on these cocktails, but I'm sure that when we get to the truth the real story will be greater than the fiction. I truly hope that bartenders will be regarded not only as professional mixologists but also historians of the art of mixing. Alchemists, yes, but intelligent gentlemen that completely comprehend the power they possess.

Over a certain number of years, I have seen some of the cocktails that I have invented in Paris adopted by my colleagues. This is a very great honour and I would like to thank those colleagues here. However, I have also seen some of my recipes appropriated or the names of the cocktails kept but the ingredients changed by different bars in order to keep costs low. That I find regrettable. Certain new cocktails, and cocktail families like the 'Perfect Cocktail' (of which more later), were invented at the Bar Hemingway, Ritz Paris: that is the fact of the matter. They will undoubtedly be made, for the great pleasure of clients all over the world, in the years to come. I would appreciate it if these cocktails' names and ingredients were respected. I ask no more than that.

This is really what has motivated me to write this book, which could equally be entitled *The Way It Was*.

'Cocktails are compounds very much used by "early birds" to fortify the inner man, and by those who like their consolations hot and strong… the cocktail is not so ancient an institution as juleps etc., but, with its next of kin, Crusta, promises to maintain its ground.' That is an extract from *Cooling Cups and Dainty Drinks*, by William Terrington, 1870.

Today there is a new cocktail euphoria arising from a sense of something being unavailable. What seems to be in short supply at the moment is intelligent imagination in cocktail creation. Anyone can invent anything, that's a fact, but the discerning clientele of today are tasting more and more expensive wines and alcohols in an in-depth exploration of new and deeper, more complex tasting experiences. These wonderful clients are offering bartenders the opportunity to create, and, quite rightly, they will not accept the mediocre. Like great sauce chefs, bartenders must be experienced and thoughtful as far as their ingredients are concerned. We must experiment with our feet on the ground and not try to create the bizarre and ridiculous in order to gain a modicum of publicity. We must work our cocktails out on paper, technically first, and then (and only then) should we produce the melange. After that, we should test it properly before our clients taste the fruit of our imagination and experience. Let's always check that the ground rules have been respected.

Now is the time to create the new cocktail age. The classic cocktails of the future are being invented today, just as the classics of yesterday were invented in Manhattan, Paris and Milan and a million other places. However, this time round let's get it straight! Let's be clear about who invented what, how, why, and when.

Contents

Introduction

The Bar Hemingway is probably one of the most important bars in the world today. *Forbes Digital Tool* Internet magazine cited it as 'The World's Greatest Bar, 1998' and its Head Bartender as 'The World's Greatest Bartender'. The author was to be cited in 2001 again by *Forbes* as the Greatest Bartender in the World. In 1983 I had obtained the title of No.2 in the world (Martini Grand Prix World Cocktail Competition) for my knowledge in cocktails and alcohols, and had coveted the premier position ever since. *Le Figaro* newspaper cited the Head Bartender as one of the 20 most creative people in France, comparing him with architects, dancers, chefs and writers. The *Times* called the Bar Hemingway the best kept secret in Paris, and compliments for our service have been bestowed upon us from all over the world. In 2001 *Le Figaro* stated that the Hemingway produced the best Dry Martini there is.

The story of the Bar Hemingway begins in 1921, when it was decided to create a room for alcoholic refreshment in the Cambon Wing. Le Café Parisien was designed in the art deco style of the period by Picot. The Head Bartender was to be Frank Meier, and he would receive the world's elite: Sir Winston Churchill, President Theodore Roosevelt, Noël Coward, Scott Fitzgerald and Cole Porter, to name but a few. It was at this time, incidentally, that Frank Meier invented the Royal Highball (a marvellously refreshing drink made with cognac, strawberries and champagne) for the King of Spain.

Just opposite the bar was a very small 'salon de correspondance' with lovely wooden walls. This became the ladies' waiting room, where ladies waiting for their husbands would while away the 'minutes'. (Ladies, at this time, were not allowed in the bars.) In 1936 the principal bar was transformed to receive both sexes, and at the same time a second bar was created. This was 'Le Petit Bar', over which Bernard 'Bertin' Azimont was to preside until his retirement in 1975. The little bar was to become Ernest Hemingway's favourite haunt. He had discovered the Ritz Paris in 1925 after meeting Scott Fitzgerald in the 'Dixies Bar', a drinking hole for ex-patriot American artists and writers. The Dixies no longer exists, but Le Petit Bar, now known as the Bar Hemingway, continues to thrive. Hemingway adopted the bar as his Head Quarters and spent many hours there planning his strategies for the horse races at Auteuil. He would even, according to A.E Hotchner's book *Papa Hemingway*, pick up the bets of Frank, George, Bertin and the other bartenders for the day's races. This was done under the profound inspiration of Bertin's Bloody Marys.

Ernest Hemingway, with his friend Colonel David Bruce (later to become the ambassador of the United States), were the first Americans to be served in the bar after the war. After hailing Sylvia Beach at Shakespeare and Co., the writer made a B-line for the cellars of the Ritz Paris. He was greeted and brought into the room now known as the Bar Hemingway (named after a suggestion from the bartender, Claude Decobert, who had served Hemingway on several occasions), where he downed 51 Dry Martinis. Incidentally, I often served Mr. Curley, in the line of American Ambassadors to have known Hemingway, at the Restaurant Au Petit Riche in 1989, but was never able to win him over to the benefits of cocktail drinking. Perhaps he too had the haunting memory of all those Martinis with Hemingway!

In 1962, Charles Ritz decided to create a third bar on the Vendôme side of the Hotel. Named The Lounge Bar, this serves an enormous daytime clientele and excels in afternoon tea and scones.

The focus on the Vendôme Bar and the absence of Bertin in the late 1970s led the Petit Bar to meander like the rivers that Ernest Hemingway had once fished upon. Its activity eventually came to a halt in the middle of the 1980s and it was used for special parties only.

With the support of Jack Hemingway, who was very favorable to its project, the Ritz Paris pushed very hard for its re-opening, and in 1994 finally offered me the opportunity to become the bartender that I had always wanted to be. (My first letter asking for a position at the Ritz Paris had been in 1979!) The Ritz Paris and I worked extremely hard to create 'The Event', the opening of the Bar Hemingway, which happily coincided with the 50 years of peace since Hemingway had liberated the bars of the Ritz Paris.

We did it! I can honestly say that I never doubted that the Bar Hemingway would be a success. In fact, in 1998 it was decided to make the bar bigger to cope with the incredible volume of new visitors. Better still (and this has to be the greatest compliment a management can offer the Head Bartender), the Ritz Paris and its entire team let me and my Number Two, Johann Burgos, design the new room. (I even found the old espadon or swordfish in the Charles Ritz Grill Room. It was no longer in use and few people ever saw it. I took it down and hung it in the Bar Hemingway.) I was pretty jolly pleased with my latest acquisition until one day, upon arrival at the Ritz Paris, I found that my (well, I *had* caught it!) espadon was now hanging upon the Espadon Restaurant, high above the door on the Vendôme side. I felt a little like Ernest Hemingway might have done had he ever experienced 'the fish that got away'!

Following page:
The plan of the Bar is very important to our regulars. This seating plan is invaluable in order to know discreetly about what's happening where and in order to maintain a modicum of reserve.

19

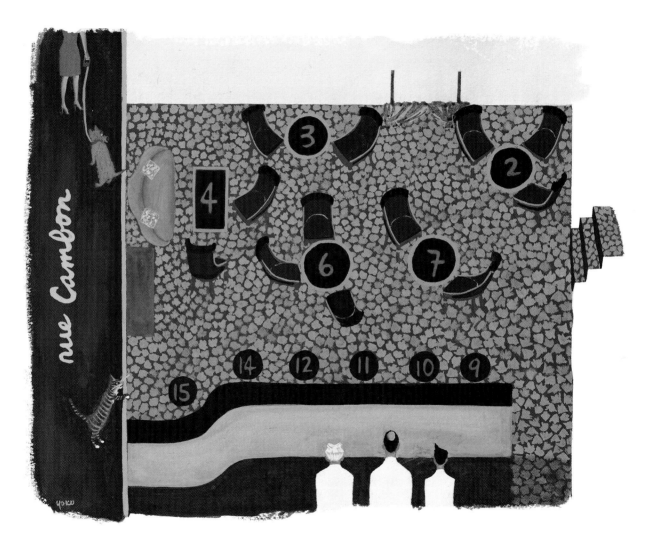

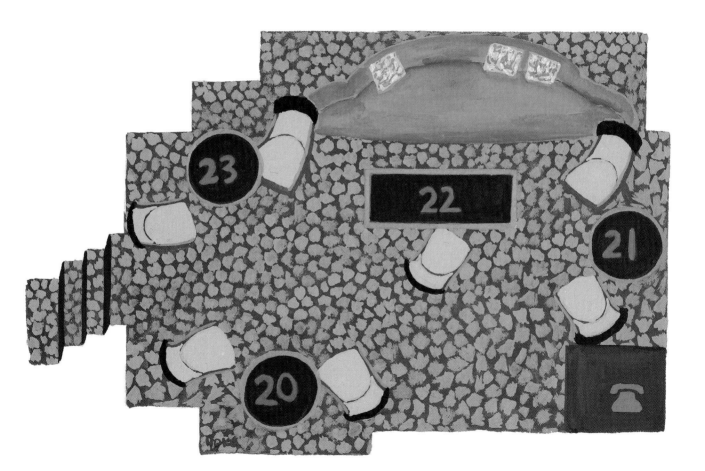

CHAPTER I

The psychology of mixing drinks

Before you set out to make a cocktail, you should ask yourself several questions:

1. Who is the person that I am making this cocktail for?

It's just like the recipe for success in any business: you have to know your customer. You have to take into account what gender they are, and what age. Young people have less drinking experience than, let's say, the over-30s. (The over-30s, with their reasonable amount of drinking experience, seem to have been on a constant quest for the drier, more simple cocktail: the ultimate is perhaps the Platinum Bullet. That's just pure gin or vodka served in a Dry Martini glass refrigerated at − 18.4 °C, with one olive and a thought for Louis Pratt. This cocktail was invented in the Bar Hemingway in 1996, but of course was inspired by the Silver Bullet.) But back to the youngsters; they go for exotic cocktails that are sweet, with lots of juices, the kind of thing you would drink by the swimming pool in Bora Bora.

Girls drink lighter than boys do. They want to drink alcohol without the taste of it and, in general, without too much of the effect. Of course, there are girls and there are girls, but one thing's for sure: saving ladies from total inebriation is an honourable endeavour.

Young men can sometimes want something powerful. Because they are young they want to feel the kick, and they would not be seen dead (in front of their pals) drinking something light. But then again, exactly which young men are we talking about? Rugby footballers at 9 o'clock in the evening or Pimm's cricketers at 5 o'clock in the afternoon? Or are they highly-stressed stock-exchange types, or the superfit local swimming team?

2. What are they celebrating?

It's very important to know what is being celebrated: the cocktail must reflect the event. As the Rank Xerox team once asked me: if the latest copier was a cocktail, what would it look like and how would it taste? How's that for a challenge? If the event is a (post-) sporting one, one has to be light and low in alcohol. If it's St.Patrick's Day, you had better use an Irish whiskey base.

Business cocktails are often vodka based (vodka based equals no bad breath, which is why Ernest Hemingway had the Bloody Mary invented for him, or so his favourite bartender said...). For business functions, the colour or the name or the ingredients of the cocktail should be relevant to the origins of the company or its president. Of course the name must have an irresistible charm about it, too.

3. What's their objective in having this cocktail?

Do they just want to have a light thirst-quenching drink, or do they want to forget a bad week? Models often like the former, although catwalk cocktails have to be short, dry and effective, to produce an instant calming effect. In this case the Kamikaze seems to rule with its reassuring mix of vodka, lemon juice and Cointreau. Needless to say, I don't know who invented it. Sometimes, of course, people just want to get drunk! (Oh, that's a horrible word! What's it doing in a book about cocktails?)

Whatever the customers' objective, you must counterbalance their prescription with what you think would be right. Two heads are better than one, especially in such a serious business as drinking.

Ritz 75

(Based on the French 75, a cocktail invented circa 1914 and named after the French 75 mm canon. It became popular in 1917 in New York in the Stork Club.)

1/10 lemon juice

1/10 freshly squeezed mandarin juice*

1 spoon of sugar

1/10 gin

champagne

Mix the lemon juice, the mandarin juice and the sugar in a tumbler. Add lots of ice. Pour the gin. Top with champagne. Garnish with slices of lime and mandarin. Add a cherry.

*The mandarin is not in the original recipe for a French 75. One can also find a dash of Pernod in some variations, and grenadine in others.

Bâtonnet

(Bar Hemingway, Ritz Paris,
26 June 2001)

1/10 cognac

4/10 white wine

5/10 tonic

2 batons of cinnamon

*Pour the ingredients into a tumbler.
Break the batons of cinnamon and
drop in the glass. Fill the glass with
ice to the top. Stir and serve.*

4. What's my objective as the creator of this cocktail?

If your customer seems flagging in energy you really ought to make a cocktail with lots of fresh juice in it. You should include sugar, a drop of alcohol and something fizzy to pep the person up, probably champagne or ginger ale. In this case, why not try the French 75, a cocktail invented in Paris (though not in the Ritz Paris) during the First World War. Incidentally, this became a very popular cocktail in the United States upon the conclusion of hostilities. We call our version a Ritz 75 as our preparation seems to be very popular and I don't want to get other bartenders in trouble.

Another cocktail, this time invented by Pauola from Argentina (a student of the Ritz Escoffier Bar classes), is perfect for a lady that would like a long drink that is refreshing but at the same time extremely light in alcohol. (This cocktail was the result of a written exercise to develop a cocktail on a hot day for a certain Elisabeth, who was also a student of the Ritz Escoffier School.)

CHAPTER II

How to prepare a cocktail

A cocktail is mixed with three different constituents: the base alcohol, the perfume and the body. One must also consider essences, as we shortly will.

The base alcohol

This refers to the alcohol from which the cocktail evolves. It is the root and stem of the mixture. Each cocktail has its solitary base; there should only be one. Mixing vodka with cognac, for example, is a technical error and a 'faute de goût'. In a Margarita, tequila is the base, whilst in a Manhattan it is the Canadian whisky.

The perfume

When you inhale the aromas of an alcohol you will be able, just as with wines, to detect the different aromatic constituents that make up the overall character of the liquid. You could, for example, have strawberry, cherry, vanilla, hazelnut or almond, apricot or prune, or possibly many of those in some combination. The professional cocktail mixer will pick out the particular aroma (which is often already in the alcohol) and enhance it with a liqueur or bitters, essences or wine-based products in order to accentuate this particular facet of the alcohol. By contrast, he may want to introduce a new perfume to the alcohol: orange and ginger, strawberry and champagne are good examples.

The body

The body is the consistency of the cocktail. One can choose between thick, thin, creamy and fizzy. Eggs and cream give thickness, while milk and egg whites give a lighter touch. Apple juice or vermouths are suitable either for clear cocktails or for those of a ruby-like appearance, and of course sodas or

champagne and beers or ciders give those fizzy, pep-up cocktails.
Here are a few examples of the above mentioned:

Base	Perfuming agent	Body
Gin	Grand Marnier	Vermouths
Vodka	Cointreau	Lillet
Rums	Amaretto	Dubonnet
Cognac	Liqueur de Cacao	Red or white wines
Tequila	Kahlua	Campari
Grappa	Fraise des Bois	Port
Marc	(strawberry liqueur)	Eggs
Brandy	Mint Liqueur	Milk
Whiskies	Benedictine	Cream
Armagnac	Crème de cassis	Fruit and vegetable juices
Calvados	Mandarine Imperiale	Consommés
Pisco	Galliano	Fresh fruit
Mezcal	Peter Heering	Marsala
Poire Williams	Apricot Liqueur	Sherries
Eau-de-vie de framboise	Peach Liqueur	Manzanilla
Kirsch	Melon Liqueur	Malaga
Quetsche	Sugar Syrups	
Vieille Prune		

Dirty Earl Grey Martini

(Bar Vendôme, Ritz Paris, 1999, Alain Willaumez)

1/10 Earl Grey tea, freshly infused a few minutes beforehand

9/10 gin or vodka

Prepare the ingredients in a mixing glass, then pour into a cocktail glass and garnish with a zest of lemon.

A note about essences

Some examples of these are raspberry, strawberry, blackcurrant, badiane or star anise, liquorice, Cassia bark, ginger, peach, Angostura bitters, orange bitters, lemon, ginseng, vanilla, nutmeg, cinnamon, truffle, fresh mint, tarragon and varied herbs, bergamot and different tea leaves. Some of these can be made through maceration in vodka or by heating in distilled water for immediate preparation. One must remember that the fruit essences used by the bartender take many months to prepare and can only be found in the elite of the world's best bars.

To take an inspirational example, Alain was my assistant whilst I was Head Bartender at the Hotel Scribe in 1987. He is now Number One Barman of the Vendôme Bar. He has always been a source of imagination and inspiration in the world of cocktail preparation and the Dirty Earl Grey Martini is one of his creations.

How the recipes are communicated internationally

In order to be perfectly understood by the world of cocktail consumers, it is very important to avoid talking in fluid ounces, gills and centilitres. If you're not from the country that uses a certain measurement system, then you're lost! Simply imagine that each cocktail is 10/10ths: whether it is a long cocktail or a short cocktail, a champagne cocktail or a double 'Old Fashioned Cocktail', its constituents will always be written in 10th parts of the cocktail. When you look at a recipe with all its measurements in 10ths, look next at the glass and imagine it separated into 10 floors. You then just follow the instructions.

CHAPTER III

The garniture

Now that the cocktail has been made, the last (and probably most important) part in its creation is the presentation. It has been said that the cocktail garniture, whilst remaining simple, should reflect one or some of the ingredients that went into the mixture (for example, the slice of pineapple on a Planters Punch). This is a very good ground rule, but it is a rule that should be developed if the bartending profession is to evolve.

Even the classic cocktails should be made to please the individual client. Although I never change the basic three ingredients of a Margarita, for example, I will make it drier for some and sweeter for others just as a tailor on a basic 48-size suit varies the arm sizes and back lengths. I also change the garnitures of my cocktails for men and women. Further still, I'll take into account how the person is dressed and whether it is day or night as part of my decision-making process.

For gentlemen, the garniture is extremely simple: a zest of orange or a slice of lemon or lime. Ladies are much more special and, just as they take care to choose the right dress, I try to choose the right garniture to go with the person, the clothes, the look or the mood. If the lady is in evening dress, a red rose should be used on the side of the glass. I like to think that, for perhaps just a few seconds, as the bartender delicately places the glass in front of the lady, the cocktail becomes part of her jewellery. The lady will feel complimented and will frequently offer the rose to her companion who, if he has a good tailor, will have the perfect buttonhole in which to wear the rose for the rest of the night. Pink roses can be used with strong colours. In springtime, yellow daffodils are very inspiring as a reminder of the season, but invariably one must counter-balance

Les tapas du Ritz changent chaque jour.

C'était bon!

C'était bon!

YOKO

the pale yellow with red fruit such as redcurrants or strawberries if possible. Of course garnishing one cocktail with an expensive rose can be... expensive! But just one petal slightly over the rim of the glass can be even more effective and very economical.

The flowers do not have to be edible. Orchids (although Scott Fitzgerald did eat a few of these in order to gain the favour of a lovely young lady in the Petit Bar of the Ritz Paris), roses, daffodils and tulips should be positioned outside of the glass. However pansies and 'fleurs de courgettes' can float in the drinks if one so wishes. These flowers are perfectly edible and have a beautiful nutty flavour that can enhance that of the cocktail.

Of course if you are doing a group cocktail at home, garniture has to stay simple, but you can still do some marvellous presentations using flower petals or different seasonal fruits.

Which garniture
Just as the great chefs de cuisine all over the world use their regional products, taking into consideration the season, a great host or bar mixologist should take into account the same criteria. Here is a seasonal guide:

- In May you can use rhubarb in your drinks and as garniture
- June is for strawberries
- July is for raspberries, cherries, redcurrants and melon
- August is for apricots and blackcurrants
- September is for tomatoes and peaches
- October is for grapes, pears, figs and apples
- In November, try horse chestnuts and pumpkins

- December to April is for vine leaves, badiane spices, cinnamon sticks, walnuts, orange peel, grapefruit and limes.

In Provence, I would work with different olive preparations. I could use star anise as well. In Normandy, I could use apples cut simply or like beautiful swans. Mushrooms, red, yellow, green and orange peppers, red chicory leaves, celery, courgettes, fresh tomatoes, lettuce leaves and even cauliflower: all can play their role, too, when making savoury cocktails. You only have to go to your local Chinese restaurant to see the beautiful sculptures in carrots and turnips that garnish your different plates to let yourself be convinced of the wonderful effects that can be created. By contrast, when I see sticks with a piece of orange and half-slice of lemon dangling around a horrific sweet cherry, creating the effect of a very dead fish, I know that efforts must be made in this area.

If you're doing exotic cocktails around the pool or you just want to evoke that kind of atmosphere, then try fresh mango and melons, goyave and coconut. The cocktail you're making, the person you're making it for and even the location you're making it in dictates the garniture that you use.

CHAPTER IV

Which glass to use

It would be very simple if we had enough money and space to have shelves all over our bar or house, holding just the right cocktail glasses for all occasions. Most of the bartenders' books I've seen have a good page of wonderful drawings of everything from liqueur glasses that look like minute sherry schooners to highball and double-highball and Collins glasses. The domestic cocktail consumers and the professional bars could easily have at least 20 or 30 glasses of each type; and that's just at the bar: we won't even go into the stock downstairs!

But, thankfully, we do not need to go to such lengths. We can do very well with just a few types of glass, and my personal despotic choice consists of four different glasses for both bar and home.

1. The tumbler or Collins glass

This is a thinner-than-usual tumbler and was possibly named after the 'Tom Collins' cocktail, which was invented in London over a hundred years ago by a headwaiter at Lammers. The Collins glass is perfect for Highballs, that is to say long drinks like gin and tonic, whisky and soda, and mojitos, the fashionable Cuban drinks. Others would include Campari and soda or Campari and orange juice (Garibaldi) gin fizzes, cobblers, coolers and juleps.

2. The Old Fashioned glass

This glass, otherwise known as the whisky glass, is very robust and you can find lovely hand-cut crystal sets that will last a lifetime at home. The glass is considered by professionals as a 'double cocktail' glass. It is not only for whisky drinking, but also for most cream drinks like the Alexander. It is also perfect for other classics like the Gin Smash and the Brandy Crusta.

3. The Bordeaux glass (also known as the Angoulême)

This glass is extremely versatile. It can be used not only for red and white wines but also for port and sherry, as well as cognac, Armagnac, whisky, calvados, liqueurs and cremes. When refrigerated, it is perfect for pear and raspberry alcohols. The Bordeaux glass suits fruit juice cocktails and exotic (a good definition of which in this context is 'by the swimming pool') cocktails like the Piña Colada or the Singapore Sling.

4. The champagne 'coupe' or cocktail glass

This is a fun glass to use. It has, however, attracted criticism because the champagne stays shallow in the coupe, and this is reckoned to suit the 'light-hearted' drinking of champagne. In the 'flute', by comparison, the bubbles take longer to come to the surface and one can examine the champagne with a more discerning eye.

The coupe is, however, a multi-use glass in comparison with its taller relation, which can serve champagne and nothing else. With the coupe, serving becomes much easier and faster as the froth doesn't inhibit quick pouring. It's also very retro (for those who like retro) and is perfect not only for party 'champagning', but also for the cocktail drink (in which I include even the Martini styles). Try the Blue Bird, the Margarita, the Manhattan and the Brandy Sangaree. The coupe is for the suave at heart. You don't believe me? *'Bond insisted on ordering Leiter's Haig-and-Haig on the rocks and then he looked carefully at the barman. "A Dry Martini", he said. "One. In a deep champagne goblet"' (Casino Royal,* by Ian Fleming, 1999).

Mojito

2 spoons of sugar

a whole stem of fresh mint

1/10 lemon juice

5/10 Cuban rum

soda

*Pour the sugar, the frest mint
and the lemon juice into
a tumbler. Muddle the whole
for about 20 seconds.
Add rum and finish with soda.
Stir and serve.*

Gin Fizz

4/10 gin

2/10 lemon juice

2 spoons of sugar

soda

*Pour the ingredients into
a shaker. Shake and pour
into a tumbler. Fill briskly
with soda.*

Tom Collins

*Exactly the same as
the Gin Fizz but built up
in the tumbler directly.*

Whisky Cobbler

2 spoons of sugar

5/10 whisky

*Pour the sugar directly into
a tumbler. Fill with broken ice
and add the whisky. Stir for
20 seconds and garnish with
fresh slices of fruit
Serve with two straws.*

Gin Rickey

the juice of half a lime

5/10 gin

soda

*Pour the gin and the lemon
juice directly into a tumbler
and drop the husk into
the glass once pressed.
Fill to the top with soda.
Add a slice of finely pared
lime peel.*

Gin Buck

4/10 gin

1/10 lemon juice

ginger ale

*Pour the gin and the lemon
juice directly into a tumbler.
Add lots of ice and fill up
with ginger ale.*

The tumbler or Collins glass ▶

Brandy Crusta

1 lemon

2 spoons of sugar

5/10 brandy

2/10 maraschino liqueur

2/10 orange Curaçao

a few dashes of lemon juice

4 drops of orange bitters

Moisten the rim of the Old Fashioned glass with a slice of lemon, then 'frost' the glass with powdered sugar from a saucer.
Cut the peel off the half-lemon spiral-fashion and lay in the glass filled with cracked ice. Pour the other ingredients into the glass.

Gin Smash

a sprig of fresh mint

2 spoons of sugar

8/10 gin

Pour the fresh mint and the sugar into an Old Fashioned glass. Muddle slightly. Pour the gin over. Add cracked ice. Stir and garnish with a slice of orange, a twist of lemon and a cherry.

Whiskey Sour

8/10 whiskey

2/10 lemon juice

2 spoons of sugar

Pour the ingredients into a shaker. Shake vigorously and pour into an Old Fashioned glass filled with ice.

Brandy Alexander

4/10 brandy

3/10 liqueur de cacao brun (chocolate/vanilla liqueur)

3/10 fresh cream

Pour the ingredients into a shaker. Shake and pour into an Old Fashioned glass.

Historical note:
the earlier version was called the 'Alexander' and the base alcohol was gin rather than brandy!

Brandy Sling

1/10 sugar dissolved in water (i.e. simple syrup)

8/10 brandy

Pour the ingredients directly into an Old Fashioned glass. Add lots of ice and a twist of lemon.

In certain recipes one will find Benedictine and bitters.

Gin Fix

2 spoons of sugar

2/10 lemon juice

7/10 gin

Pour the ingredients directly into an Old Fashioned glass. Add cracked ice and stir. Garnish with seasonal fruits and the peel of the lemon.

The Old Fashioned glass ▶

Brandy Alexander

Yoko

Piña Colada

yoko

Piña Colada

4/10 white rum
2/10 coconut milk
1/10 fresh cream
3/10 pineapple juice

*Pour the ingredients directly
into a shaker. Shake well
for 9 seconds or put into
an electric blender for
the same amount of time.
Pour into a Bordeaux glass
and garnish with a slice of
pineapple and a slice of apple
and a cherry that has
macerated in eau-de-vie.
Serve with straws.*

Singapore Sling

4/10 gin
1/10 cherry brandy
1/10 lemon juice
1 spoon of sugar
(or no sugar, and just add
Benedictine and bitters)
soda

*Pour the gin, the cherry
brandy, the lemon juice
and the sugar into a shaker.
Shake well and serve into
a Bordeaux glass and fill with
ice and soda. Garnish with
fruits in season and serve
with straws.*

Daiquiri

First, a little note on its origins, with an extract from *The Gentleman's Companion*, 1946, by Charles H. Baker Jr: 'The two originators were my friend Harry E. Stout, now domiciled in Englewood, New Jersey, and a mining engineer associate, Mr. Jennings Cox. Time: summer of 1898. Place: Daiquiri, a village near Santiago and the Bacardi plant, Cuba. Hence the name.' Now that's a well-referenced cocktail!

5/10 Bacardi rum
3/10 lemon juice
2/10 sugar cane syrup

*Pour the ingredients into a shaker.
Shake and pour into a Bordeaux glass 'straight up'
(meaning no ice) or into an Old Fashioned glass with ice.*

Manhattan

(Attributed to Jenny Churchill, the mother of Sir Winston Churchill)

7/10 Canadian whisky

3/10 red vermouth

a few drops of angostura bitters

1 cherry in eau-de-vie

Pour the ingredients into a mixing glass then into a cocktail glass and drop in a cherry in eau-de-vie. If you use a stick to hold the cherry, make sure the end of the stick passes the glass by at least 1 1/4 inch.

Millionnaire

(Hotel Ritz London, no later than 1922)

---

the white of a fresh egg

2 dashes of Curaçao

1/6 gill of grenadine

2/6 gill of Rye Whisky

Fill the shaker half full of broken ice and add the ingredients. Shake well and strain into a cocktail glass. A dash of absinthe may be added if required.

*Please note that in this recipe, I have had to use the 'gill' measurement, despite my recommendation about always using tenths, as it is not of my invention.

Margarita

5/10 tequila

2/10 Triple Sec (Cointreau)

3/10 lemon juice

Pour the ingredients into a shaker. Shake and serve in a salt frosted cocktail glass. No garniture.

Brandy Sangaree

8/10 brandy

2/10 port

Pour the brandy directly into the cocktail glass filled up with cracked ice. Float the port over the top with a bartender spoon. Serve.

▶ The champagne 'coupe' or cocktail glass

Sticks and Things

Let's not muddle up pretty cocktails for little children – you know the ones; they're garnished with monkeys climbing up sticks, beautifully painted parrots, umbrellas and frozen pink elephants for ice cubes – with adult cocktails. Of course, there's nothing wrong with them, and anything that delights a child is fine by me: they just do not belong in a professional bar.

There are, however, some incredibly super sticks that look great in certain cocktails. They can reflect a topic, excite the drinker, offer an occasion to collect (as we all know, people love to collect things) or publicise a brand or company. I'm thinking of the Jim Beam Mexican Cowboy, the Get 27 green bottle stick, or the Ballentines swordstick. All of those really look great in different cocktails, as do the naked mermaids (they belong to no particular drinks brand at all, but – let's face it – it's always agreeable to find a naked mermaid in your glass!)

The latest fashion in the top bars of the world is the crystal stick. It may be the latest fashion, but this style has been around for years; perhaps it's just starting to be appreciated by the general public (maybe a little too appreciated, as the sticks are disappearing at a phenomenal rate).

I would like to see more publicity sticks with imagination behind them. And why not in wood, too? If oak is good enough to age fine spirits all over the world for two, four, twelve and forty years, surely wooden sculpted sticks couldn't harm a cocktail in half an hour! The possibilities are quite interesting for this style of artisanal expression, as long, of course, as the final result enhances the cocktail.

CHAPTER V

Cocktails and the stories
that belong to them

Midnight Moon (Suzanna)

(Hotel Scribe, 1982, all rights reserved by the author)
A cocktail for the end of the evening.

1/10 cognac

1/10 Amaretto

1/10 liqueur de cacao blanc (white chocolate liqueur)

champagne

Fill the champagne coupe, preferably refreshed in your freezer, with all the ingredients to a half-inch from the top. Drop a small zest of orange into the glass. Garnish with a half-slice of apple cut into the shape of a half-moon and placed onto the glass.

The Midnight Moon was created at the Hotel Scribe in 1982, during my time as Assistant Head Bartender.

To give a precise time would be difficult, but just after the 17th May would be pretty correct.

A beautiful blonde young lady around my age (I was 21 that day) walked into the bar, which was named Le Bar St. Laurent. This vision was followed by another beauty! As usual myself and my bartender colleagues looked at each other with a plea stated so often that it had now become telepathic: 'I hope she asks for me'.

As it was my birthday, I was hoping that someone was smiling upon me that night. I'd been obliged to come into work, but, come to think of it, where better place to be on your 21st birthday than in a beautiful Parisian bar?

One of the ladies, looking a bit dreamy (Oh God!) said, 'We're looking for Colin, Colin Field, a bartender here'. (Oh God! Oh God!) Somehow managing not to faint, I introduced myself, and Suzanna and her friend explained that they were working in The Plaza Hotel Hamburg with my sister and they had brought my birthday presents. I offered the girls a cocktail or two (I hope my old Head Bartender never hears of this) and then, after work, Suzanna and I (her friend had left for an important rendezvous) went for a late dinner in an old restaurant in rue Mansart called La Cloche d'Or. The next day Suzanna left Paris and I never saw her again.

The Midnight Moon is golden like Suzanna's hair and tastes of Lubeck Marzipan, one of the finest, sweetest things to come from Germany.

56

Amaretto
Story of a liqueur.

There is a marvellous story about Amaretto that is influenced by Chaucer's *Canterbury Tales*. Our story is called 'The Franklin's Tale'.

Dorigan, a beautiful young maiden, is soon to wed a marvellous young knight called Arveragus. Unfortunately, Arveragus has to go and fight in the Holy Wars, but he is fortified by the promise that Dorigan will await his return and then they will marry. Enter Aurelius, a young knight that comes upon this beautiful, untouchable, young lady... and falls in love with her.

Aurelius decides after a long period of chivalrous 'attente' to approach Dorigan and let her know of his 'pains of the heart'. Being a well-brought-up maiden, she tries very hard to think of a noble solution to the problem; she advises Aurelius to go away and perform knightly deeds, killing armies, wolves, dragons, a few wicked giants, a couple of witches and some nasty men. (She is secretly hoping that by that time Arveragus will be back.)

Not quite. Aurelius goes forth, and in just one year succeeds in working through the list, motivated by the great love he possesses for Dorigan. Dorigan is now confronted by a knight of great worth, who is good-looking, courageous and with a certain net value (although his stock is not as high as that of Arveragus, who is fighting with the King). But then Arveragus hasn't sent any word of his adventures! No news, no nothing. Is he still alive? Oh! What is a poor young maid to do? She tells Aurelius that LOVE is the most important sentiment in life and that, despite the heroic valour of his deeds, she does not love him.

Aurelius goes away, sick to the soul. He wastes away for two years, pale and with no will to live. His brother hears of his calamity and comes to call. He sees a man, decimated by an unrequited love. So, after a great deal of thought, the brother decides to offer a desperate piece of advice: consult the witch! She could, perhaps, find the solution. The price (almost certain to be everything Aurelius owns) would be on the high side. But Aurelius is desperate, so, he goes down to the witch with his brother and with his ill-fitting armour, his sword and lance, his shield and his colours. He also drags along all the gold he still has, the titles of his castle, the lot.

The witch (no supermodel, but a true professional) listens patiently to his problem and measures the weight of the task that she has been proposed. The work involved is far greater than the modest wealth of this courageous knight and she tells him that he cannot possibly afford her expertise. Assailed by one disappointment too many, Aurelius finally breaks down. Worrying that Aurelius might take his life, the brother offers the money to complement the great debt that would be owed to the witch. This, the witch takes and decides to help him (no discounts, you understand: it will still cost him everything he owns and the brother's fortune, too).

She gives him a small bottle of a potion with instructions on the side of the bottle. Aurelius follows them to the letter and then asks to be accepted by Dorigan. The Lady acquiesces and Aurelius repeats the exact speech the witch has told him: 'Dorigan, I accept that you will never love me for there is someone else in your heart. Let us drink this farewell glass of friendship and you shall be rid of me forever'.

Dorigan accepts, hoping that she will be rid of this young man's intents forever, but, after just one sip of this potion, she looks upon this admirable person that has obviously given his very soul for her love and realises that she has made a terrible mistake... She instantly falls in love with Aurelius and they get married and live happily ever after.

The Italian name of this potion? Amaretto. So the moral is: consume, or prepare, with moderation!

Ritz Pimm's

(Bar Hemingway, Ritz Paris, August 1994)
Excellent from 11 in the morning to late summer evening aperitifs in the garden.

1/10 the alcohol base desired
1/10 dry vermouth
1/10 Martini Rosso
1/10 Campari
1/10 Dubonnet
1/10 ginger ale
10 drops of angostura bitters
4/10 champagne
a slice of apple
a slice of pear
slices of orange and lemon,
plus zests
5 or 6 green grapes
2 or 3 black grapes

Pour the ingredients into a crystal beer pint glass. Add the fruits and garnish with 2 whole sprigs of fresh mint (cut the ends off).

Although the recipe was really put together by myself at the Warwick Hotel in 1983, it was never truly perfected until I had access to all the fruits imaginable in the Ritz Paris. Only then could this cocktail become a Ritz Pimm's.

Note that a Ritz Pimm's will be always preceded by the alcohol preference: gin, whisky, vodka, cognac, etc.

I often put in strawberries and raspberries with some redcurrants, which do nothing really for the taste, but do enhance the presentation. For the ladies, I add a few petals of a rose or an iris flower whole. I also use a very long piece of cucumber cut on the skin.

Ritz Pimms

Miss Bonde

(Bar Hemingway, Ritz Paris, December 1994)
An elegant aperitif cocktail for beautiful ladies.

In the opening days of the Bar Hemingway, it was frequented by a young inter-national elite. That is one of the reasons for its success today. Its clientele consisted of gentlemen and ladies, under 25 years old for the most part, of the very highest education and order. These key people were the backbone and advocates of the Bar Hemingway; they were my best clients and my most frightful critics: the gentlemen pulled no punches in voicing their disapproval of any action on my behalf that wasn't to their taste.

Just as there were the 'Bentley Boys' in the 1920s, these gentlemen I called 'The Ritz Boys'. They all have their favourite cocktail, but, knowing them, they would all prefer that I mentioned one that I invented for two sisters who were friends of them all.

1/10 raspberry vodka
champagne

Pour the raspberry vodka into a champagne coupe straight out of the freezer and fill with champagne. Garnish with a rose.

To prepare raspberry vodka:

8 3/4 oz. raspberries
a bottle of Absolut vodka

Drop the raspberries one-by-one into a bottle of vodka (or, if you prefer, 3/10 of the bottle). Wait for three weeks and serve at − 18.4 °C into a frosted cocktail glass.

Highland Cream

(Bar St. Laurent, Hotel Scribe, September 1982. Ritz Paris reserves all rights to this cocktail).
An end of evening creamy night-cap.

1/10 Grants blended Scottish
whisky
2/10 coffee liqueur
2/10 crème de cacao brun
1/10 black espresso coffee
4/10 crème fraiche

*Pour a shaker filled 2/3 with ice
with all the ingredients.
Serve in an Old Fashioned glass
or in a cocktail glass.
Garnish with a little chocolate
powder and serve.*

In the early 1980s there had been a fashion for a certain pre-prepared cream liqueur. A great deal of bartenders in the area didn't seem to put this creamy pre-prepared drink in fridges, but rather left the bottle on the shelf. The dilemma was one of product visibility: if the client didn't see the product he wouldn't buy it! The problem was that, between you and me, this cream product was, once opened, still on the room-temperature shelf for up to a week or (dare I say) much longer! Although I am very sure that the public health propriety of these pre-prepared products was above all reproach, let the facts be known! I decided that I would prefer to make these cocktails myself.

This raised another constant question for the people that work in the drinks profession: was I just a drink pourer or was I a Professional Bartender? If you go to a restaurant and order vegetable soup, do you expect the chef to open a tin and heat the contents, or do you expect him to peel the potatoes and dice the carrots, before dropping them gently into a casserole of fond de bœuf and bubbling water? You prefer the latter? Of course you do...

The Highland Cream took me six months to perfect in 1982. It has become over the years one of my signature cocktails. Every time it has been served, the mixture was only seconds old. The bar of the Scribe over which I presided no longer exists. A few years after I left that lovely bar it was transformed into a smaller open salon.

The Dry Martini - My Story

Every bartender has a theory about the world's most famous cocktail. I feel that this is the true story.

I believe that there are two serious elements that are to be taken into account: the ever-rising popularity of gin and its seeds of noblesse from the 1860s. (It was now being sipped, instead of being guzzled, in all parts of the British Empire.) Coupled with that is the popularity of mixed drinks, juleps, cups and cocktails in the United States from exactly the same period. We are, in effect, tracing an evolution from the Jerry Thomas sweet 'Martinez Cocktail' coupled with the very English and comparatively dry Plymouth 'gin cocktail'. (Plymouth gin is relatively sweet for a gin of today), to the replacement of the 'Martinez Cocktail' by the 'Martini Cocktail'.

The Dry Martini Cocktail, the history of gin and the story of the British Soldier cannot be disassociated, even though the origins of Genievre are well proven to be Rotterdam. Key factors in the origins of 'The Dry Martini' are English social and economic evolution. Its fame, however, is a result of the status it achieved in the United States, in and out of Hollywood, as a result of the Volstead Act (Prohibition). One must also not forget the immense contribution offered by our British, very British, James Bond as well as the literary contributions by writers like Somerset Maugham and our beloved Mrs. Beeton, (*Mrs. Beeton's Book of Household Management, London, 1906*).

It might well have been the gin of Lucas Bols that the English soldiers tasted whilst fighting in numerous religious and political conflicts between the 16th and 17th centuries. They were probably seeking that 'Dutch Courage', as any wound could prove fatal in these pre-antibiotic times. This was a period when one would lift one's glass and toast 'Your health, Sir!' and really mean it. The British soldier was not able to enjoy ale or brandy and therefore he adopted gin. Gin (or, at least, the rudimentary principles of its distillation) was brought to England around this time.

In 1688 the Protestant William and Mary of the Netherlands were invited by the English Parliament to accept the throne and replace the Catholic James II, who had fled to France. The period during and after such upheaval always causes a form of social depression: as so often, alcohol lightened the working man's burden. Then, taxes were increased on French brandy whilst favouring the distillation of gin. This in turn caused huge benefits for the English landowners' grain sales.

By 1733 gin was in! Certain people even received part of their pay in the form of this 'noble' alcohol (which was not always so nobly distilled). By 1734 drunkenness began to alarm the wealthier citizens, who were beginning to fear mob riots. In 1738, the first of many Gin Acts was passed, putting prohibitive taxes on the gallon of gin. The result for the unfortunate Prime Minister Walpole was inadvertently to start a race to make even more gin!

All these laws were repealed and reinvented in 1743, then in 1751. Drunkenness was still a problem; consumption still remained at around 11 million gallons a year in England. Illness, disease, riots, murder and theft were rife, and gin was at the core of the problems, as we can see from the writings of Fielding and the paintings of Hogarth, such as 'Gin Lane'. Gin became known as the 'mother's ruin' as excessive consumption and base methods of distillation could render people impotent.

By the 1800s the dark Gin Hole gave way to the Gin Palaces. The Industrial Revolution was underway. Thousands of country people poured into London for work and a better standard of living. Overseas, the British Army was all

YOKO

over the world guarding the empire, and so was the Englishman's alcohol.

The paradox of the 'Gin Revolution', the working man's (or, frequently, non-working man's) poison, is that it was vilified while playing a big role in the new world's social activities. Rudyard Kipling summed up the cultural divide that could create such a paradox: 'The civilian who'd be delightful if he had the military man's knowledge of the world and style, and the military man who'd be adorable if he had the civilian's culture' (*The Education of Otis Yeere,* 1889).

The Dry Martini as we know it today was being drunk well before the Dry Martini of the 1920s and onwards. The true origins, although very evident to the British historian (which I do not have any pretensions of being!), lie in British colonialism, the history of which is full of adventure and heroics. How can we have all forgotten those British Grenadier Guards marching through India and Africa? Gin, although the working man's burden and the educated man's tipple was, above all else, the Navy and Military officer's friend (along with rum for the lower ranks).

The British Empire was expanding and glorifying herself through the courage of the British Soldier. In the Indes, Egypt, the Sudan, Burma, the Northwest frontier, Rhodesia, West and South Africa, the Guards, the Lancers, the Fusiliers, Dragoon Guards, Kings Royal Rifle Corps, Argyll and Sutherland, York and Lancaster were fighting in their squares.

'At Rorke's Drift, against the brave and courageous Zulus, the 24th Regiment, the 2nd Warwickshire's, fought valiantly with 'Henry-Martini' rifles towards yet another victory. I would just like to add, having been born in Warwickshire, myself, that, contrary to popular belief, there were just as many Englishmen, Scotsmen and Irishmen as there were Welshmen in that particular skirmish, not to mention a Swiss or two and at least 1 Scandinavian!' (Ian Knight, *The Defence of Rorke's Drift,* 1999)

The alcohols they were drinking next to their single shot Martini Rifles were gin and perhaps some rum.

" 'Put your hand under the camel bags and tell me what you feel'. I felt the butt of a Martini and another and another. "Twenty of 'em", said Dravot placidly. "Twenty of 'em and ammunition to correspond"…"Heaven help you if you are caught with those things!" I said. "A Martini is worth her weight in silver among the Pathans" ' (Rudyard Kipling, The Man Who Would Be King, 1889.)

The man behind the Martini-Henry Rifle, known simply as the Martini, was Friedrich Chevalier de Martini of Frauenfield in Switzerland. He was the inventor of the Martini breech action, which, with Alexander Henry's rifling, made the most important contribution to troops all over the world from 1869 all the way to 1920. Compared with, say, the Spitfire of the Second World War and its short life, one can see how deeply rooted the Martini .40 and .303 rifles were in the hearts of the British trooper. It can also be said that a great deal of cocktails were inspired by wars in general! Here are two examples: the Whiz-Bang and the Depth Bomb.

'Five volleys plunged the files in banked smoke impenetrable to the eye, and the bullets began to take ground twenty or thirty yards in front of the firers, as the weight of the bayonet dragged down, and to the right arms wearied with holding the kick of the leaping Martini' (Rudyard Kipling, The Drums of the Fore and Aft, 1889)

Glasses of gin were being drunk by the British troops in 1870. Indeed, Noilly Pratt reinforced with gin was being consumed at the same time; perhaps the evil taste of badly distilled gin was offset by the addition of vermouth. At any rate, people were experimenting. They were mixing the gin with their bitters, orange bitters or angostura bitters, calling it either the 'Gin Cocktail', or, later on, the 'Pink Gin'.

In all honesty, one can trace in *The Savoy Cocktail Book*, 1930, almost a genus of Martinez Cocktails: there's the Martinez 'Third Degree' with absinthe, olive, gin and French vermouth. Then there's the 'Fourth Degree' cocktail (also considered a Martinez), consisting as it does of gin, French vermouth and Cinzano. A cherry is used for garnish. In the 1887 edition *Bartenders' Guide* by Jerry Thomas, one finds that both the Manhattan and the Martinez cocktails both have maraschino in them, are both shaken and poured into a 'small bar glass'. After the Martinez Jerry Thomas goes on to recommend a 'large cocktail glass'. That excepted, we have our good old Martini and Manhattan of today.

By 1895 in George Kappeler's *Modern American Drinks* the Martini is well established, the maraschino having been replaced by a maraschino cherry 'if desired by customer'.

I mentioned two elements that were to be taken into account in the birth of the Dry Martini. However, there is also room to consider the Martini Rossi claim that Martinis were named after their company: Kappeler's book mentions 'Italian vermouth' for both Martinis and Manhattans, and cites several examples in the 1920s of a Martini cocktail having to have 'Martini' vermouth in it.

Depth Bomb

A cocktail for before dinner.

Owing its inspiration to the M.L. Submarine Chasers during the First World War (*The Savoy Cocktail Book*, 1930).

1 gill* of brandy

1 gill* of Apple-Jack brandy

1 teaspoon of grenadine

2 teaspoons of fresh lemon juice

Fill the shaker half full of cracked ice and add all the ingredients. Serve in a cocktail glass.

Whiz-Bang

(Recipe by Tommy Burton, Sport's Club, London, 1920)
A cocktail for the aperitif.

The cocktail is named after the high velocity shells so-called by the Tommies during the war, because all you heard was a whiz and the explosion of the shell immediately afterwards.

2 dashes of orange bitters

2 dashes of grenadine

2 dashes of absinthe

1/6 gill of French vermouth

2/6 gill of Scotch whisky

Fill a bar glass full of crushed ice and add all the ingredients. Stir up well and strain into a cocktail glass. Squeeze lemon-peel on top.

*Please note that in these two recipes, I have had to use the 'gill' measurement, despite my recommendation about always using tenths, as they are not of my invention.

The world's first Dry Martini without alcohol!

In view of increasing accidents on the roads and more and more strict laws concerning 'drinking and driving', one would think that a bartender's scope is getting horrendously narrow. On the contrary: as bartenders we have a major responsibility towards our customers. We should spend a little time (or even a lot) trying to find new drinks that can enhance a party without pushing our guests 'over the top'. Here at the Bar Hemingway we have been working on the New Dry Martini for over two years with just that purpose in mind. What is a Martini without alcohol? You may well ask.

We have made a drink that has the lovely bouquet of juniper berries, is totally dry, and attacks quite lightly the palate and warms the throat as the Martini changes temperature and descends into your soul. It does everything a Dry Martini does for you: the only thing is that alcohol will not filter into your blood. You might still want to drink a real Martini, but who's to stop you having two or three New Age Martinis afterwards, just to stay with the party?

The Georges Cocktail

(Invented in Cognac, 1997, a Bar Hemingway cocktail)
An early evening aperitif.

4/10 Remy Martin V.S.O.P. Cognac
1/10 Stones ginger wine
(a very important ingredient
at 12° abv.)
5/10 tonic water

*Pour the ingredients directly
in a tumbler filled with ice.
Garnish with very thin pieces
of lemon and orange.*

This cocktail is for two gentlemen named Georges. One is Georges Clot, the 'Maître de Chai' of Remy Martin, the man that puts together Louis XIII (is Louis XIII Georges or is Georges Louis XIII?). The other is Georges, the great one-time Head Bartender of the Ritz Paris. Georges Clot is a man of great integrity, a man of very fine taste and an absolutely superb dining friend. We have spent many hours together talking of our passions, me with a certain vibrant electricity and Georges with an almost Buddhist Zen aura that is calming and appealing. He's a superb diplomat in company, remaining modest and never taking the stage, and yet you know that he has the answers to all your questions before you even ask them. Georges and I beg to differ only on one topic regarding cognac cocktails. Georges likes cognac over ice in a tall glass, topped up with tonic water; I find that drink horrendous! You see, the quinine in the tonic overpowers the cognac. But Georges is steadfast and so I've 'arranged' (slightly) his cocktail so that he can still follow his basic recipe.

Georges Scheuer was the bartender of the Ritz Paris between 1926 and 1947 and Head Bartender until 1969. He was the precursor of the modern true Head Bartender and my model as Head Bartender of the Bar Hemingway. He did not just serve drinks: he was a friend to his guests. He would welcome certain guests at the entrance of the hotel, not hesitating to take their baggage up to the room. He would also enjoy accompanying, when he was free to do so, his guests to the exit of the Ritz Paris to say goodbye at the end of their stay, and this is something I also do.

More than just a bartender (if I may use that phrase about one of the noblest callings a man can have), Georges was a personal friend for his clients. Today I too enjoy an extremely friendly relationship with my guests. We will regularly go clay pigeon shooting or just enjoy a barbeque in my own garden. Friendship has always been a question of respect. I treat my guests in the Bar in the same way I would treat them in my own home, and vice versa.

La Crevasse

(Bar Hemingway, Ritz Paris, 1998)
A delicious end of evening cocktail after a night at a play or the opera.

This was invented for Vladimir Volkoff when I had read his book *La Crevasse*. The garniture presentation is influenced by the book cover. Monsieur Volkoff has been a great adept of this cocktail, as is his daughter. I'm still working on another cocktail to go with his latest book, *Il y a Longtemps, Mon Amour*.

1/10 raspberry vodka
(see the recipe p. 65)
1/10 pear liqueur
1 dash of wild strawberry liqueur
champagne

Pour the raspberry vodka and the liqueurs directly into a very cold champagne flute. Fill with champagne. The garniture is non-obligatory for the novice and primary for the professional.

Benderitter

(Bar Hemingway, Ritz Paris, 1995)

The Benderitter is the precursor of a new genre of cocktails, the 'Perfect Cocktails'. These can be consumed both before and after the meal!

1/10 ginger essences

champagne

Pour the ginger essences into a frozen champagne coupe. Fill with very cold champagne. A small slice of kumquat should be dropped into the glass, although my ghost won't haunt you if you use a zest of orange.

To prepare the ginger essences:

vodka

ginger root

In a small bottle filled 7/10 with vodka, add a handful of skinned ginger. Forget about it in a cupboard (not in the fridge) for 2 months. Shake it from time to time. You now have ginger essences.

It's 5:30 in the afternoon. One of the chefs of the restaurant, Jean-François Girardin, has more than too much ginger root. 'Colin', he called, 'try doing something with this!' I wasn't too keen, but Monsieur Girardin was most insistent and the challenge was too much for me, so my mind went to work on the best utilisation of this new produce. A couple of hours later a friend of mine, Brigitte Benderitter, the public relations expert of the French publishers Gallimard, walked into the Bar Hemingway. She tasted, as a guinea pig, my latest formulae and pronounced it her cocktail! I couldn't acquiesce: Brigitte had been a friend over several years, first coming into my life in L'Hotel, rue des Beaux-Arts, where I had been Head Bartender and Restaurant Manager and Banquet Manager (all that was covered by the term 'Head Barman'). But even so, how could I call a cocktail either the 'Brigitte' or 'The Benderitter'? Brigitte was adamant, and didn't play fair: she reserved the Bar for all of her journalist friends, and they all had the same instructions: they could drink what they liked, but if it wasn't the Benderitter Cocktail, they had to pay for it!

Needless to say, this very personal signature cocktail is now called 'Le Benderitter' and the desire to authenticate its pedigree is a major reason for writing this book. Too many stories are flying around and too many artists are trying to sign the sculpture!

Ritzini

(Bar Hemingway, Ritz Paris, 1994)
A Martini-style 'Perfect Cocktail'.

8/10 vodka

2/10 ginger vodka

(see the recipe p. 80)

Pour the ingredients into a mixing glass filled with ice. Stir the cocktail for 10 seconds and pour into a cocktail glass.

Working with the 'ginger in vodka' maceration, this easy cocktail popped out quite naturally. This is a cocktail belonging to the 'Perfect Cocktails' genre as it can be drunk at the beginning of a meal and at the end.

Ross d'Ecosse

(Hotel Scribe, 1982, all rights reserved)
A dry aperitif cocktail but also a nice end of evening drink belonging to the 'Perfect Cocktail' family.

1/10 single malt whisky

(Cardhu for example, as it is light but with lots of character)

1/10 mandarine imperiale liqueur

Pour the whisky and the mandarine liqueur into a chilled champagne flute. Fill the flute to the top with fresh and ice cold champagne. Decorate with a lovely rose cut 2 1/2 inches down on the stem.

This was named after a very lovely and intelligent Moulin Rouge, M.G.M., and later Lido dancer whose proud origins were Scots. As Ross was her name, the bartender played with the words Rose of Scotland and Ross of Scotland, as this lady represented everything that was beautiful in that country. To echo the lady herself, he made a blonde cocktail with a classic presentation, rather intrepid, with a marvellous Highland perfume. He was destined (or doomed) to serve this cocktail in every bar he worked in order to remember her forever.

Serendipiti

(Bar Hemingway, Ritz Paris, 1994)

An all-evening cocktail, particularly in hot weather.

This was invented for Jean-Louis Constanza. Jean-Louis first came into the Hemingway Bar on 31 December 1994. A great sportsman, he is a successful businessman and devoted Epicurean. He loves to experiment in the world of mixed drinks and has already four or five cocktails to his name. We worked this one out together one evening in the Bar while he was waiting for friends. Upon tasting it, Jean-Louis exclaimed 'Serendipiti'! I asked him what that beautiful word meant. Apparently it means 'when you find what you've always been looking for, without knowing that you had been looking for it'. This instantly became the name of the cocktail. Although many people have adopted this cocktail and possibly even drink it more often than Jean-Louis himself does, I say again: Let The Truth Be Known!

one sprig of mint

1/10 calvados

2/10 apple juice

champagne

In a tumbler, take one full sprig of mint, cut the bottom of the stalk off and place the sprig in the glass. Add the calvados and muddle the two ingredients together, only slightly bruising the mint. Add plenty of ice cubes and the apple juice. Fill almost to the brim with champagne. Taste and say 'Serendipiti'!

Ritz Cider

(Bar Hemingway, Ritz Paris, 1996)

An afternoon or early evening cocktail.

This is actually an intermediary step towards the Serendipiti cocktail. I was trying to make a cocktail that was very light in alcohol for ladies that wanted a cocktail but without the taste of alcohol.

5/10 apple juice

5/10 champagne

Pour the ingredients into a Bordeaux glass filled with 3 large lumps of ice. Garnish with a very thin slice of apple dropped into the glass, or add a white rose petal to the surface of the mixed drink.

Mach 2 (Landsberg)

(Bar Hemingway, Ritz Paris, 1995)
A cigar cocktail.

1/10 ginger essence
(see the recipe p. 80)
3/10 green Chartreuse
6/10 Scotch whisky

*Pour the ingredients into
an Old Fashioned glass.*

The roots of this cocktail go back to Christmas 1981, while I was studying English Literature and History in Tresham College in England. I tasted in the local pub a marvellous mixture called a 'Whisky Mac', a simple cocktail consisting of: 4/10 Stones Ginger Wine to 6/10 Scotch whisky, served in infinitely small doses.

In 1985, whilst working at the Mercure Montmartre Hotel, I started mixing whisky with green Chartreuse, but it wasn't until 1997 that the missing ingredient came to me. Philippe Landsberg, a training consultant and strong cigar smoker, asked me for a cocktail to go with the last one-third of the cigar. The 'Purin', as a friend from Switzerland would say, is the best and most powerful part of the cigar. One needs a cocktail that would complement the earthy coffee-and-black-chocolate taste.

The secret of a successful cocktail is to reproduce the taste associations that people are already mildly familiar with and the different flavours that come through the cigar.

Back to the Mach: I came up with the punning 'Mach 2' because I had so obviously been influenced by the Whisky Mac, and, of course, the power reference relates to the speed of sound.

Kashenka

(Bar Hemingway, Ritz Paris, 1996)
A dry middle of the evening cocktail.

This was named after a very pretty Polish cabaret dancer that worked in Paris in 1991, not far from the Ritz Paris. Her true name was Catherine, of which the friendly diminutive is Kashenka. This cocktail was invented for her.

4-5 strawberries
2 teaspoons of white castor sugar
Polish vodka

Remove the leaves and put strawberries into a large Old Fashioned glass. Add the sugar and apply enough pressure on the fruit so as to slightly bleed them without crushing them. Add largely cracked ice all the way to the top. Pour in Polish vodka and stir gently. Garnish with a red rose petal.

Violaine

(Bar Hemingway, Ritz Paris, 1998)
An elegant late soirée cocktail.

Mr. Norbert Kneip is one of the most perfect bar persons I can imagine. A retired professor of literature, his object in life is to find food of great character and refreshing personalities. His official residence, written on his visiting card, is 'The Bar Hemingway Paris' and he indeed receives all the people important to him at the Bar. Taking a Heineken to refresh himself before a very dry Manhattan 'with just a drop of vermouth for the colour, Colin', he will then proceed to entertain the guests all over the Bar with his experience and wealth of culture.

Norbert appreciates most particularly an actress of great potential who acts in plays by Stéphane Gildas. She has been to the Bar many times in the company of Mr. Kneip; he asked me to create a cocktail for her.

1/10 pear alcohol
1/10 wild strawberry liqueur
champagne

Pour the pear alcohol and the wild strawberry liqueur in a champagne coupe. Fill with champagne and garnish with a red rose.

Limoncello 'di Piave', code name: Lemon Charlie

(Bar Hemingway, Ritz Paris, 1999)
A pleasant cocktail for the aperitif or for after the meal.

5/10 Limoncello di Piave

5/10 Smirnoff Black vodka

Pour the ingredients directly into a cocktail glass. Garnish with a red rose on the edge of the glass for ladies.

This is a bartender's 'Limoncello' that is basically made on the spot. I named it 'di Piave' after Hemingway's First World War injury at Fossalta di Piave. Upon serving it to a very pretty top English model (let's just call her 'Kate'), the name was rectified to Lemon Charlie. 'Kate' has been a true friend of the Bar. Every time she is in Paris she'll bring all her friends along and we'll have a terrific party. I have also on occasion made cocktails for her at her own parties in England and have heard her talk very positively of our cocktails.

One needs to prepare, with a bottle of grappa, the skins of three beautiful lemons (just the yellow of the skin, not the white, as this will make the grappa sour). The preparation needs to be aged for at least eight weeks. Then add some filtered lemon juice and sugar.

Once the preparation is ready, keep it in a freezer. Take it out 20 minutes before pouring.

Meloncolin Baby

(Bar Hemingway, Ritz Paris, December 1996)
A cocktail for all the soirée.

1/3 of an Ogan melon
1 spoon of sugar
vodka

Put the melon's pulp into an Old Fashioned glass. Add the sugar and slightly muddle the two ingredients together without crushing the melon. Fill the glass with lots of cracked ice. Pour in the vodka to taste. Stir and drop in the glass a small segment of the husk of the melon.

Melon is a very difficult product to work with and, invariably, once added to alcohol becomes overly sweet.

One fine night, very, very late at the Bar Hemingway, some dear friends from New York, Bridgitte and John, were having a splendid time. I really don't remember who invented the cocktail, but it started as 'Melon Baby', which became 'Meloncholy Baby' and then 'Meloncolin Baby'.

Le Loup fera nid

(Bar Hemingway, Ritz Paris, 1994-2000)
A summertime cocktail, very Martini style and delightfully refreshing.

---

10 oz. of watermelon
(crush the watermelon and extract just the juice)
or 3/10 water-melon juice
7/10 gin

Pour the ingredients into a shaker. Shake and serve in a cocktail glass. No garniture.

One of my guests – let's call him Nicolas – has been a faithful friend of the Bar Hemingway. He has introduced so many people to my team and me that his membership card (these are extremely difficult to obtain) is marked Number One out of 47 members.

Over the years he has tasted many successful cocktails that I have invented for his friends. But he always wanted his own special cocktail. He always has had his special cocktail, too, but, just as one gets tired of one's aftershave, my friend tends to tire of his cocktail and, although the name never changes, the cocktail is in constant evolution! Here is today's recipe.

Meloncolin Baby

Yoko

P.A.S.S.

(Bar Hemingway, Ritz Paris, 1996)
A cocktail for the aperitif or for refreshment as a digestive.

Mr. Peter Smith, an English man 'cap a pied' and regular visitor to the Bar Hemingway, discovered this cocktail in a restaurant in France. After the help of restaurateurs and bartenders in England and France in 'rounding off the corners', he has adopted this cocktail and made it his own. He has enthusiastically proposed it to all his guests, who invariably have at least one. Although one could imagine this as an aperitif cocktail, Mr. Smith habitually drinks it around midnight on Friday nights.

4/10 vodka

2/10 grapefruit juice

3/10 champagne

1/10 cassis

Pour the vodka, the grapefruit juice and the champagne directly into an Old Fashioned glass filled with ice. Pour the cassis generously over the ice cubes. Garnish with a blackberry.

Clockwork Orange

(Bar Hemingway, Ritz Paris, 2001)
A cocktail for long aperitifs.

Another such cocktail would be the Clockwork Orange, which was invented for a young lady called Frankie.

The mixed drink is almost a 2001 Screwdriver, and Frankie, a lovely lady from the United States, very much enjoys this particular potion.

1 orange

2 spoons of sugar

5/10 Smirnoff Black vodka

In an Old Fashioned glass, crush pieces of orange with the sugar. Add cracked ice to the top and add the vodka.

Fiesta

(Bar Hemingway, Ritz Paris, 1997)
A cocktail for parties.

5/10 fridge cold Cointreau

1/10 grenadine

3/10 vodka

1/10 Campari

In a shot glass (which is not one of the four glasses that I recommend in this book), pour first the Cointreau, then the grenadine, which will sink to the bottom. In a mixing glass, marry the vodka and the Campari. Pour gently over a spoon on top of the Cointreau. You now have red-white-red cocktail.

This is the kind of cocktail the French call a 'pousse-café', as it has several levels. It is said that Frank Meier would not employ a bartender unless he was quite familiar with rainbow-like pousse-café. In the United States it might be referred to as a shooter, which means that one drinks it all in one go!

The Fiesta was invented to celebrate the 70 years since the publishing of *The Sun Also Rises* or *Fiesta*, the only Hemingway book to have two titles. In 1997 we had a terrific party at the Hotel, with over 300 people in celebration. The Fiesta cocktail is red-white-red, designed like that just to say that the sun also rises.

Think of Pamplona and San Sebastian. Think of Duff Twysden, Hadley Richardson and Ernest Hemingway. Drink this cocktail whenever you're depressed and please do remember: the sun also rises.

Bière Ritz

(Bar Hemingway, Ritz Paris, April 1998)
An afternoon and all evening cocktail.

5/10 beer (a light beer)

5/10 champagne

Pour the ingredients into a beer glass. No garniture.

This is a rare occasion where, having been given a name for a cocktail by Richard Pearson, an international lawyer and friend (and absolutely 'the man to know' in Paris), I decided to invent the cocktail around it: the word-play was so irresistible, and Biarritz was the place most of the elite were going to at that time.

Zelda

(Bar Hemingway, Ritz Paris, 25 August 1994)
A devilishly mad aperitif cocktail.

6/10 tequila
4/10 lemon juice
2 drops of Pili Pili (devil
peppers macerated in vodka)

Pour the ingredients into a shaker.
Serve in a cocktail glass.

Something mad (rather like Scot Fitzgerald's wife, Zelda) that I invented on the opening of the Bar Hemingway. I got the idea from a visit in a Tex-Mex restaurant. The more I ate those tortilla chips with that delicious tomato dip, the more I wanted to eat more tortilla chips with that delicious tomato dip. That's not fair! With the Zelda cocktail, the more you drink, the more you're thirsty.

Recently I found my cocktail recipe in a supermarket magazine that dated the cocktail to the 1930s! If I didn't set the book right now, I'm sure I'd be deprived of my invention: by the way, I'm only 39 years old!

Apple Pilar

(Bar Hemingway, Ritz Paris, August 1994)
An excellent business aperitif and, dare I say, a marvellous children's
afternoon refreshment.

1 sprig of fresh mint
1 spoon of sugar
4/10 apple juice
ginger ale

Pour the ingredients directly into
a tumbler. Muddle lightly and
add ice. Finish with ginger ale.

One of our non-alcoholic beverages, this was named after Ernest Hemingway's favourite fishing boat (which can still be seen in Cuba). I wanted to create a drink that was refreshing and clear without all those fruit juices mixed together, and this is greatly appreciated by American officials of the highest calibre.

Cognac aux Truffes

Le Cognac aux Truffes

(Bar Hemingway, Ritz Paris, February 2000, Christophe Léger)
*This cocktail is the perfect cigar cocktail after a perfect
'high-level gastronomy' meal.*

Christophe, the No. 3 of our team, had been experimenting with all manner of macerations. A great many, although worthy of encouragement, were, unfortunately, frightful. Undaunted, he started to work on the maceration of truffles from the Dordogne area of France with Armagnac. Slowly he found that cognac carried the perfume of the truffle better. This very unique mélange has taken Paris by storm and numerous articles can be found mentioning this superb cigar-friendly preparation. It also introduces a seasonal aspect into the world of cocktails, as the truffle is only available for part of the year. As we are a very small bar, we cannot prepare too many bottles of this very magic potion. For me this is one of the greatest contributions to the world of French cuisine since the Port Wine cocktail and I take this preparation very seriously. It is also interesting to note that different truffles give slightly different tastes and definitely different perfumes. This makes the discovery of different bottles of Cognac aux Truffes even more fascinating. Unique to the Ritz Paris and marvellously typical of the quality of the bartenders of the Hotel, this preparation shows that the world of cocktails is in constant evolution.

We have tried several cognacs and have found that Hennessy X.O. Cognac is absolutely exquisite with this preparation.

Serve to cigar lovers and precious friends.

1.5 oz. diced truffle

1 bottle of Hennessy X.O. Cognac

*Let the truffles macerate one month
in the bottle of cognac.
Serve in a Bordeaux glass.*

Lutteur III Horses Neck

(Bar Hemingway, Ritz Paris, 1998)
Early evening long drink cocktail.

1 orange

2 drops of angostura bitters

4/10 Hennessy V.S.O.P.

6/10 Schweppes ginger ale

In a tumbler, hold up with ice the rind of an orange. Pour the other ingredients into the glass and serve.

Lutteur III. Born in 1904 of Saint Damien and Lausanne. Trained by Mr. Batchelor and Mr. Escott. A horse. Lutteur III was the property of Mr. James Hennessy of Hennessy Cognac. Lutteur III won the Grand National Steeple Chase, the greatest horse race in the world, on 26 March 1909. The jockey was Georges Parfrement. Mr. Parfrement offered France her first victory at the Grand National, and he had only visited the racecourse for the first time the day before!

Georges Parfrement talked to Hemingway years later. He had said that the true danger in a steeplechase is not the obstacles but rather the horses' pace. (Georges Parfrement was to kill himself in a benign horse race in Enghien on the last jump, a jump that was only three feet high.)

A friend of mine that enjoys cognac cocktails was absolutely delighted when I came up with this cocktail. I was, of course, playing with the idea of the 'Horses Neck' cocktail. Francis suggested that I should use a complete orange rind rather than a lemon. This cocktail is the preferred drink today of Gilles Hennessy.

The Wood Cocktail

(Bar Hemingway, Ritz Paris, 1997)
A cigar cocktail.

Hemingway enjoyed shooting and often trained at the Cazadores Club in Cuba with clays and pigeons. Over the years working in the Bar Hemingway, the virus has got to me, too. As a very keen sporting clay and skeet shooter and the occasional woodcock and snipe shooter in Northern Ireland, I have a lovely collection of hunting guns, including a beautiful Damascus, hammer action, circa 1923, which I use regularly.

This is one of my favourite whisky cocktails for the end of the evening. The idea came to me after whisky tasting with Philippe Faure-Brac, who, among many other accolades, was named the best Sommelier in the world in 1992. We were both in the same team for a *GaultMillau* blind tasting and the orange and chocolate came over very strongly; we knew immediately that this was the Aberlour 15-year-old.

During my time in Ireland, I only had the Bushmills and found that the cocktail still worked marvellously and even 'felt right' whilst I was in Northern Ireland at very low temperatures. By the way, one of the most fabulous ways of eating porridge before your bacon and eggs is with 1 fl. oz. Bushmills whiskey, 3/4 fl. oz. pasteurised cream and fine Demmerera sugar over the hot porridge. I shall never eat porridge any other way from now on. Famous Grouse is another whisky of my choice because it's my favourite blend and has the best name for a game bird shooting cocktail!

8/10 Famous Grouse blended whisky or Bushmills Black Irish whiskey or Aberlour 15-year-old
1/10 liqueur de cacao blanc
1/10 Curaçao

Pour the ingredients into a mixing glass. Blend and pour into a cocktail glass.

Raspberry Beret or Raspberry Martini

(Bar Hemingway, Ritz Paris, 1998)
A Martini cocktail perfect for the beginning of the evening or as a refreshing digestive (which puts this into the category of 'Perfect Cocktails').

10/10 raspberry vodka
(see the recipe p. 65)

Serve the raspberry vodka at – 18.4 °C in a cocktail glass.

This cocktail is an extremely popular Martini. The colour is absolutely amazing, almost fluorescent pink. The Bar tends to serve several bottles of this elixir every evening. This, of course, forces me to have a stock of over 40 quarts continually ageing in the Spanish *solera* method. The older product helps to age a slightly younger product. (The name Raspberry Beret comes from one of the bartenders singing a Prince song as he was serving it.)

The Stanford Cocktail

(Bar Hemingway, Ritz Paris, 4th February 2000)
An excellent aperitif cocktail, which also goes very well with the new, younger cigars from Cuba, not to mention those from the Dominican Republic.

4/10 cognac
6/10 Amontillado sherry
1 dash of angostura

Pour the ingredients into an Old Fashioned glass. Stir and serve.

One of my patrons, Patrick Perreault, has become, over the last year, a great ambassador of our little bar. He has always carefully selected those people he wished to invite and has been a pleasure to serve on each visit. To commemorate his acceptance at Stanford University, I invented this cocktail. It's a very 1920s style cocktail, indeed it's a good cigar cocktail, too. (Patrick doesn't smoke cigars... yet.)

The Picasso Martini

(Bar Hemingway, Ritz Paris, 14th October 2000 at 1:45 am)
A cocktail for twelve o'clock.

No, Picasso never drank this cocktail. Of course, the great man was famous for many styles of artistic expression, including Cubism. Cubism was developed around 1906-7, and Picasso's *Les Demoiselles d'Avignon* probably marks the beginning of the movement. Through neo-Cézanne, Braque and Juan Gris we get to Synthetic Cubism around 1914. Cubism was all about the reduction of something to its essence, a kind of mechanical breaking down of a subject. This is my 'broken down' Martini.

The idea came from two lovely American ladies actually drinking Benderitters in the Bar. We were talking about making home Martinis, and one of the ladies talked about ice cubes at the same time as the other was talking about Noilly Pratt. I was in the middle listening to both of them and I heard the message: Noilly Pratt ice cubes! Brilliant! The do-it-yourself Martini. The bartender puts in the cube just before serving the cocktail and five seconds later the client takes it out or leaves it in.

For perfect dryness, if desired, ensure that the temperature of the dry vermouth is less than that of the gin in order to avoid unnecessary melting.

In order to make a Noilly Pratt ice cube one must reduce the alcohol content of this dry vermouth with distilled water to 5° abv. Exactly. I use a relatively inexpensive Vinometre, usually used for verifying the alcohol content of wines. The effect is very artistic, new wave, 'Non dit'. Keep the cube in until the perfect balance between gin and vermouth is obtained.

8/10 gin at – 18.4 °C degrees
1 cube of Noilly Pratt

Pour the gin into a cocktail glass. Take out your frozen Noilly Pratt cube and drop it into the glass.

a full sprig of fresh mint

3 Barman spoons of white castor sugar

1/10 lemon juice

4/10 Makers Mark bourbon whiskey

5/10 pumpkin juice

Pour directly the fresh mint, the sugar and the lemon juice into an Old Fashioned glass. Muddle the ingredients together for 10 seconds, no longer. Add the whiskey and the pumpkin juice. Stir and serve with a black straw and enjoy this treat!

The Pumpkin Cocktail or the Fonseca?
The Headless Horseman or The Jack O'Lantern?

(Bar Hemingway, Ritz Paris, 2000)

A cigar cocktail. Try a Romeo y Julieta Cazadores with this marvellously refreshing half-mojito, half-mint julep cocktail.

This is a super Halloween Franco-American cocktail, to be served through the month of October and, for those that missed out, occasionally in November, too. Dominique Fonseca and I invented the Pumpkin Cocktail. Dominique has been with the Hotel for over 20 years, and in 2000 received the highest award a French chef can obtain, Meilleur Ouvrier de France. I spoke with Dominique about the problems I was facing with the pumpkin, and it was due to this famous Ritz Paris chef's enthusiasm and wise suggestions (and also those of Johann Burgos, my Number Two) that I managed to create this jewel in the crown.

2 drops of Lapostolle cognac

2 drops of Grand Marnier

2 drops of wild strawberry liqueur

2 drops of port

1 cinnamon stick

slice of orange and lemon

red wine

Pour the ingredients into a wine glass. Fill with hot wine and wait 5 minutes before serving.

Hemingway Hot Wine

(In our Bar since 1994)

Each year in England on 5 November, we burn Guy Fawkes. This rather unpleasant 17th-century fellow wanted to blow up our Parliament. These days, it's the day in the year when we all look at spectacular fireworks displays on a cold English night. My mother, Renate, who is of German origin, used to make a hot wine for all the family that allowed us to keep the cold out.

After some years' experience at the Bar, I've got the know-how to improve upon the recipe.

yoko

Dakota

(Bar Hemingway, Ritz Paris, March 2000)
A sportsperson's drink, or for the businessperson on the go.

Whilst in the R.A.F in the 1940s, my father's favourite plane amongst all the Lancasters and Wellingtons was… the Dakota.

4/10 Smirnoff vodka

3/10 carrot juice

3/10 beef consommé

condiments (salt, peper, Tabasco, Worcestershire sauce)

Pour the ingredients directly into a tumbler. Shake and serve. Garnish with celery stick.

Platinum Bullet

(Bar Hemingway, Ritz Paris, 1997)
A cocktail from twelve o'clock.

Upon reading a gentleman's book on Dry Martinis, I asked myself how I could do a 'one up' on that famous Silver Bullet Dry Martini. And I love the name. I'm quite sure that the Dry Martini was invented by the English around 1869 and named after that superb Martini-Henry rifle that was so efficient for the Royal Engineers in the latter part of the 19th century. So there you have it: a Platinum Bullet is even more rare and valuable than its silver cousin!

'Dry Martinis are always too cold when they are served and too warm when I finish them' (Paul Newman at the Bar Hemingway in 1999.)

Tanqueray gin at − 18.4 °C degrees

Pour the gin directly into a cocktail glass refregerated at − 18.4 °C. Add a very large non-tinned olive and toast the Royal Engineers!

The City

(Bar Hemingway, Ritz Paris, 19 May 2000)
A Martini-style drink.

8/10 raspberry vodka
(see the recipe p. 65)
1/10 the juice squeezed from half
a lime
1/10 Cointreau

Pour the ingredients directly into a shaker. Serve in a cocktail glass. No garniture.

Lucas Zachara, one of the faithful clients of the Bar Hemingway since 1994, has always been a Martini drinker.

Recently, he changed towards Cosmopolitan cocktails, but found them too sweet and lacking that marvellous Martini kick. We soon remedied the situation with this cocktail.

Tützins

(Bar Hemingway, Ritz Paris, 1995)
An early evening cocktail after a long day.

1/10 scotch whisky
1/20 Kummel liqueur
Tütz Beer

Pour the scotch and the liqueur into a beer glass. Fill to the brim with freezing cold beer.

Marie Lauren Muller of the Schutzenburger brewery once asked me to invent a cocktail with her Tütz Beer.

As usual, I took my time over it. The cumin in the Kummel liqueur that I use flavours this beer nicely. The name is a slight deformation of the word *Totsins*, a sort of 'until we meet again' in the Afrikaner language (a nod to my father, who was born in Cape Town).

ice brewed beer since 1740

thtz

la bière la plus fraîche du monde

yoko

Bilbo Baggins

(Bar Hemingway, Ritz Paris, 1994)
A potent end-of-dinner drink.

6/10 Pisco Control

4/10 Cointreau

Pour the ingredients directly into an Old Fashioned glass filled with ice. No garniture: it just looks like a glass of water!

Bearing in mind the Bar Hemingway's great literary associations, I couldn't resist squeezing in my all-time favourite adventure books, *The Hobbit* and *The Lord of the Rings* by Professor J.R.R. Tolkien. *The Hobbit* started to be written in around 1930, and Hemingway, who would have been in his early thirties at the time, would certainly have appreciated this book of adventure, courage and endeavour.

Bilbo Baggins is the book's original hero (though it's Frodo who goes on in the true family spirit to save the world). None of this swashbuckling is very 'hobbit-like'. Hobbits are peaceful creatures who do not like habits to change or adventures to happen, so the cocktail I've invented is just what Bilbo would need if he had killed a dragon, fallen down the stairs or forgotten the biscuits for tea!

Fratini

(Bar Hemingway, Ritz Paris, 1994)
A potent end-of-dinner drink.

5-8 strawberries

of the very best quality

vodka

Leave the strawberries inside a vodka bottle. Wait 3 weeks and serve over ice or prepared Martini fashion.

Again an easy preparation, invented for my own pleasure...

116

Le Charray

(Bar Hemingway, Ritz Paris, 1999)
An aperitif cocktail.

'Le Comte de Charray', is a marvellous client to have in the Bar. His wit, humour and public schoolboy charm seems to 'create the moment' for people from all over the world in the Bar. Unfortunately, his domain in the Ardèche places great demands on his time and we do not see him as often as we would like.

One evening 'Monsieur le Comte' was evaluating the possibilities of growing wine on his vast domain and enjoying a nice fresh glass of crisp Sancerre, when I decided to go a step further. With the Count's permission, and remaining very conservative, I tried reinforcing the Sancerre with a mystelle (a grape juice that has had its fermentation stopped by adjunction of alcohol). Lillet is from the Bordeaux area. It is a marvellous aperitif on its own and is also ideal for cocktails as it already has an alcoholic base. Monsieur le Comte decided a little later to add one drop of angostura bitters to my recipe and today drinks nothing else; neither do his friends. Several hotels have already called me up for the recipe. I think that Monsieur le Comte and myself both enjoy the publicity.

3/10 lillet

7/10 white dry wine from France

1 drop of angostura bitters

Pour the ingredients directly into a Bordeaux glass. No garniture for gentlemen and a white rose on the edge of the glass for ladies.

CHAPTER VI

Cigar cocktails

What is a cigar cocktail?

It is paramount to understand the different types of cigars before one even attempts to create these very specific and technical recipes. Some cigars are strong and earthy with that marvellous smell of the countryside. Other types are the smooth and chocolate 'Ramon Allones' or 'Rafael Gonzales'. Then there are the light and fruity, vanilla, walnut and herbal tastes offered by the 'Gloria Cubana' modules, or the vegetal characters of the 'Hoyo de Monterey No. 2'.

Cigar vintages change as the factories change, and each year seems to offer a new venue. The tobacco plants themselves are indeed developing. The more stable anti-Black Shank and Blue mould disease 'Habana 92' plant and the 'Habana 2000' plant are changing the tastes and ageing qualities of today's cigars. Experiments with the new 'Habana Vuelta Arriba' plant are also very successful against the Broomrape and Mosaic disease. On the one hand, the harvests are more reliable; on the other, so it is said, the cigars do not age for so long as before. Around ten years is the maximum today, as opposed to 20-30 years in the 1960s. Not that there is a great problem: it is as difficult to get a 10-year-old cigar as it is to get a 2-year-old. I've found the average age of the cigars bought in the shops around six months!

One factor that is totally neglected is that the cigar manufacturers are changing each year; the last Romeo y Julieta Cazadores that you enjoyed might have been made by one of twelve different factories in 1998 (José Marti, Briones Montoto, Villa Clara, Sancti Spiritus and Pinar del Rio, to name but a few). Some of these very same factories are also making Cohiba, H. Upmann, Partagas, Punch and, well, just about everything except Cifuentes (which stopped production in 1985).

In order to create cigar cocktails, it is very important to smoke cigars oneself. The bartender or cocktail amateur must have, therefore, an up-to-date knowledge of the cigars that he is serving. Is this realistic? Of course it is. When you ask the wine butler or his recommendations, you quite correctly assume that he has a privileged knowledge of the product that he is proposing you.

There are many adjectives to describe the different experiences on the palate a cigar can offer. It is vital to know and understand the development of the smoking experience before any attempts can be made to conjugate a suitable cocktail. One will find out very quickly that no one cocktail goes with a cigar. (Maybe there is an exception to this rule in the Dominican Republic cigars. There is very little development through the cigar. Such cigars are termed linear. As the taste hardly changes through the cigar, the same cocktail can be appreciated all the way through.)

The Havana cigars, on the other hand, vary not only from box to box, but from cigar to cigar. Not only that: the quality of the rolling leaves (if you'll allow the play on words) much to be desired. I would definitely recommend that the Havana cigar smoker should select Robustos, Gran Coronas, Coronas Gordas like the Juan Lopez No.1 and Monte Cristo Series No.2, often called T or Torpedo, and the Belicosos of different factories.

The ventilation of these cigars is 90 per cent perfect and, as a Head Bartender who cuts about 20 cigars a day, I get to cut a very wide choice bought in France, Spain, England and Switzerland. I am adamant that the quality in England and in Switzerland is far superior to that in the rest of Europe. It's a question of maturing these cigars. Whatever the inconveniences may be, the quality of good cigars in the future lies in a greater care of stocking and bringing out these marvellous symbols of Cuban artistry a little bit later than we do today. This is where the non-Havanas are gaining an enormous amount of ground. Their reliability and quality of manufacture is far superior. The serious cigar smoker would be ill-advised not to carry a good Davidoff, Flor de Selva or Hoya de Nicaragua in his cigar case: it might just save the night!

France has a superb choice of cigars. However, the connoisseur should consider the majority as 'Primeurs', like wines to be stocked and aged. That said, the 'Beaujolais Nouveau' has a worldwide following and so should young cigars have.

The ageing of well-rolled cigars is a marvellous experience. To buy a young cabinet and, from time to time, take out an example, to estimate its development and then bring it out on a special occasion, knowing perfectly the level of perfection whilst one's guests appreciate this superb 'vitole', is truly the measure of an Epicurean connoisseur.

To analyse the Havana cigar
The Havana cigar however can be separated into three distinct thirds:
The beginning, where the cigar just warms up. The cigar will taste quite light and its personality will not yet be affirmed. There will be a light vegetal taste; perhaps the taste of autumn wet hay and an ever-so-faint hint of mushrooms of the fields. The second part of the cigar is the more balanced part. The chocolate, roasted coffee, earth, vanilla, ginger, light spices, nutmeg and cinnamon. The second part of the cigar is balanced between the lightness of the beginning of the smoke and the strength of the last third. The last third is the most appreciated by the true cigar lover. This is where the strength of the cigar lies. The strong black chocolate and deeply burnt coffee seeping through the waves of coriander and curried spices, black crushed peppercorns and Tabasco invading the palate and kissing the lips at each encounter. This is where the cigar smoker must strategically count the spaces between each draw or the cigar will get too hot to

be able to appreciate these last 'senteurs' of an often all-too-short marvellous relationship between the master and his cigar.

As one can see, it would be vain to try to make a cocktail with any kind of comparative panoply of tastes from start to finish. Either the bartender must choose the part of the cigar he would like most to compliment or (forever the salesman) must make two or three cocktails to accompagny the hour's relaxation. It is for the bartender and the experience his palate has formed on the stronger alcohols to produce the melanges to go with the cigar.

Cigar odours and how to get around them for the happiness of the majority
Candles are the best solution, but one has to choose the right scent. The best candles (with not more than 7 per cent of perfume) would be those that enhance the essences that the cigar aficionado is enjoying. One should try chocolate, vanilla, walnut, roasted coffee, ginger and nutmeg and cinnamon. These essences will render the cigar smoker's presence more palatable to his non-smoking company whilst he is enjoying the perfect end to a perfect (or otherwise) night. These perfumes are perfectly adapted to the cigar smoker and possibly could enhance his enjoyment or even enhance the cigar he is smoking at the time. One will often find that the day after a pipe smoker has filled the room with his burning tobacco, the odour of raisins and chocolate is quite agreeable.

P and T

(Bar Hemingway, Ritz Paris, 31 December 1999. Invented by Johann for Philip and Thomas. Made famous by Pierre and a lot of his friends who, I dare say, have made the cocktail well known in the Bar).
A cigar cocktail.

Philip and Thomas are two American gentlemen who come to the Bar Hemingway New Year's Eve Party. As well as champagne, they love vodka cocktails. About 4 in the morning, Johann concocted this Brazilian-influenced cocktail, which is just like the Caiparinha, and yet completely different! A friend of the Bar Hemingway met these gentlemen, and every time he comes to the Bar he drinks one of these, toasting absent friends. He enjoys smoking Hoyo de Monterey Double Coronas or for a slightly stronger taste, depending on the age of the cigars, a Punch Double Corona, Cabinet Selection of 50 'de preference'.

1 lime cut into wedges
1 lemon cut into wedges
2/10 Cointreau
8/10 vodka

Put the lime and the lemon directly into an Old Fashioned glass. Crush until the juice rides over the segments. Add broken but not crushed ice (too much water in crushed ice). Pour the Cointreau and the gin. Stir gently and serve. No garniture as the colours of green and yellow from within are quite enough.

The Burgos

(Bar Hemingway, Ritz Paris, September 1995)
A cigar cocktail.

6 drops of angostura bitters

9/10 cognac

Pour the ingredients directly into an Old Fashioned glass filled with ice. Stir and serve.

Johann and I had had an exhausting night. It was 5 o'clock in the morning, we had just finished clearing up and we sat down and opened the chessboard. We both chose a nice cigar and I proceeded to get thrashed by Johann, as usual. Chess has been an enigma to me: it's the only game I thoroughly appreciate whilst always losing!

This is when I thought of the cocktail to go with our cigars. Named after Johann, it's 'rapid and efficient' like the man himself.

No Name

(Johann Burgos, Bar Hemingway, Ritz Paris, 2000)
A very good cigar cocktail for the middle of the evening.

8/10 aged rum

2/10 honey

4 batons of cinnamon, broken in halves

Pour the ingredients directly into a shaker. Shake vigorously and serve in a cocktail glass. No garniture.

This is Johann's cocktail, an almost brutal immediate maceration of cinnamon in a teaspoon of honey with rum.

Johann invented this cocktail whilst tasting Bacardi Spice Rum. He immediately recognised the different spices, and particularly the notes of cinnamon. He set off on a way of producing this fine rum himself and after a few trials came up with this extremely fashionable cocktail. I hate to say it, but the cocktail is technically correct and is perfectly harmonious in its melange. Not only that, but it is regularly ordered by the 'alumni' of the Bar.

No.1

(Bar Hemingway, Ritz Paris, 24 July 2000)
A very good cocktail from eleven o' clock in the morning when the weather is warm.

Upon finding a new herb – Lemon Verveine – in the Chefs' fridges, I was immediately inspired. I invented this cocktail for myself and for the cigars that I was smoking at the time, Nat Sherman Gotham Selection No. 500.

Why did I call it 'No. 1'? Because it was my favourite summer cocktail. I would be dreaming about this mouth-watering delight whilst I was in the south of France and unfortunately not able to find lemon verveine!

1 whole sprig of fresh lemon verveine

2 spoons of sugar

1/10 Perrier

plain Absolut vodka

Pour the lemon verveine, the sugar and the Perrier directly into an Old Fashioned glass. Muddle slightly the verveine branch. Fill with cracked ice, not machine powdered ice as this melts too quickly and sheds too much water.
Fill up the glass with vodka.
The taste of this lemon herb vodka is absolutely superb.

CHAPTER VII

Cocktails that have been invented over the years in the Ritz Paris, the Cambon Bar

(usually known as the Ritz Paris Bar)

Blue Bird

(Cambon Bar, Frank Meier, 1933)

This cocktail was invented for Sir Malcolm Campbell to celebrate the land speed record. Today the bartenders tend to use blue Curaçao for the colour, although this, of course, is quite incorrect.

8/10 gin
2/10 lemon juice
a few drops of blue vegetable dye

Pour the ingredients directly into an Old Fashioned glass.

Nicky's Fizz

(Cambon Bar, Franck Meier, 1923)

Specially made for Prince Nicolas Toumanoff.

1/2 glass of sweetened grapefruit juice
1 glass of gin
Schweppes soda water or siphon

Pour the grapefruit juice and the gin into a shaker.
Shake well and strain into a tumbler. Add Schweppes soda water or siphon and serve.

Sea Pea

(Cambon Bar, Frank Meier, 1933)

Invented for Cole Porter, a regular of the Cambon Bar and friend of Frank.

3/10 anis
1/10 lemon juice
tonic

Pour the anis and the lemon juice directly into a tumbler.
Fill with tonic.

Elegant

(Cambon Bar, Frank Meier, 1933)

Grand Marnier was a liqueur often used in the Ritz Paris. Indeed Cesar Ritz was very friendly with the Lapostolle Company, to whom he had given the idea many years before that they should call their Marnier Orange Liqueur 'Grand Marnier'.

5/10 gin
4/10 dry vermouth
1/10 Grand Marnier

Pour the ingredients directly into a mixing glass. Stir well and pour into a cocktail glass.

N.C.R.

(Cambon Bar, Frank Meier, 1933)

This was a special for the National Cash Register Company!

1/3 Noilly Pratt vermouth
1/3 crème de cacao
1/3 rum

Pour the ingredients directly into a shaker. Shake well and serve in a cocktail glass.

Green Hat

(Bar Cambon, 1933)

1/2 glass of gin
1/2 glass green crème de menthe
a split of Schweppes soda water

Pour the ingredients directly into a tumbler with a large piece of ice. Stir and serve.

Corpse Reviver N°2
(Cambon Bar, Frank Meier, circa 1926)

Mr. Newman, Head Bartender of the Grand Hotel, one of the older cocktail bars in Paris, had already noted a Corpse Reviver in 1909. The cocktail recipe is therefore Frank Meier's, but the generic term 'Corpse Reviver' belongs to another era.

juice of one quarter lemon

1 glass of Pernod fils anis

champagne

Pour the lemon juice and the anis in a champagne coupe with a piece of ice. Fill with champagne. Stir and serve.

Mimosa
(Frank Meier, 1925, apparently)

I have read in a few books that we actually invented the Mimosa in 1925 at the Ritz Paris. However, in Frank Meier's book of 1933 he cites the Mimosa or Champagne Orange and does not sign it himself. Can it be safe to assume that the Ritz Paris did not invent this cocktail? Did Frank forget to sign his creation?

juice of one-half orange

champagne

Pour the orange juice into a champagne coupe with a piece of ice. Fill with champagne, stir and serve.

Fog Horn
(Cambon Bar, 1933)

1 glass of gin

ginger beer

Pour the gin and a large piece of ice into a tumbler. Fill with ginger beer, add a slice of lemon and serve.

Death in the Gulf Stream

(Hotel Ritz London, not later than 1922)
A cocktail from eleven o'clock in the morning.

The last of these cocktails is one that I definitely have not invented. It's called 'Death in the Gulf Stream', and was invented by Ernest Hemingway himself in January 1937 in Key West (according to *A Gentleman's Companion* by Charles H. Baker Jr., second edition, 1946).

'Take a tall thin water tumbler and fill it with finely cracked ice. Lace this broken debris with four good purple splashes of angostura, add the juice and crushed peel of one green lime and fill glass almost full with Holland Gin... no sugar, no fancying. It's strong, it's bitter, but so is English ale strong and bitter, in many cases. We don't add sugar to ale, and we don't need sugar in a Death in the Gulf Stream... or at least not more than 1 tsp. Its tartness and its bitterness are its chief charm. It is reviving and refreshing; it cools the blood and inspires renewed interest in food, companions and life'.

Epilogue

So I have come to the end of this little jewel for everyone's pleasure. The greatest pleasure has been for me, of course. Certain facts have needed to be stated and perhaps a few legends brought into perspective. It's not 35 years after a cocktail has been invented that one finally owns up!

Every cocktail in this book that has been invented by me is signed. The other cocktails are described and assigned with the greatest amount of truth possible. I have tried to cite my sources whenever possible. The classic cocktails, for the glass examples, have no stories attached for the most part.

Of course this book had to be written. The contribution to the world of cocktails that the Bar Hemingway has made is immense. Whenever you see in a world-class bar those lovely pieces of fruit and ice cubes in a simple glass of water with a lovely cocktail garnished with a rose or an orchid, spare a thought for the Ritz Paris Hemingway bartenders. Shot down in flames years ago, we forced up the standard and today our method is adopted in many top bars.

By all means, enjoy bartenders' cocktails all over the world, but take a brief second to see who is in front of you. It's all part of the game, and cocktails can be as fun as they are very, very serious.

Thank you for indulging me. I have wanted to write this book for many years but never really dared. I'm not a writer and although I have so many things to say, so many theories to propose and defend, I've always been worried about the way I would communicate them on paper. I hope that this little book will offer you many hours of enjoyment and will be your friend in many situations, especially those that call for the right cocktail.

One must always remember to keep one's cocktails as simple as possible and as technically correct as possible. Do not mix grape alcohol with grain alcohol unless you can justify your decision, an error that even the greatest houses can make in an effort to create sales. Cocktails are great fun but those that make them must take their preparation very seriously; otherwise, they will fail. Make sure you have lots of ice, a good shaker, the right glasses, sticks and fruit to garnish. Make sure that if you're making lots of cocktails that you are free of any other pressing business as you will be completely absorbed in the making of the drinks with no time for anything else.

Colin Peter Field

Acknowledgments

A special thought to Brigitte Benderitter,
who really has been my friend
in this venture.
Many thanks also to Fernando,
'intrepid barman' of the Hennessy Group.
Many thanks to the two barmen
Johann Burgos and Christophe Léger
for their efficiency, their sense of humour
and their patience with regard to me.
Thanks to my friend Yoko,
the illustrator of this book, who followed
me in all the little details.

Cocktail Index

SIMON & SCHUSTER
Rockfeller Center
1230 Avenue of the Americas
New York, NY 10020

French translation copyright © 2001 by Editions du Chêne
Copyright © 2003 by Editions du Chêne
All rights reserved, including thr right of reproduction
in whole or in part in any form.

First Simon & Schuster edition 2003
Originally published in France in 2001 by Le Chêne as
Les Cocktails du Ritz Paris.

SIMON & SCHUSTER and colophon are registered trademarks
of Simon & Schuster, Inc.

For Information about special discounts for bulk purchases,
please contact Simon & Schuster Special Sales:
1-800-456-6798
or business@simonandschuster.com.

3   5   7   9   10   8   6   4   2

Library of Congress Cataloging-in-Publication Data is available.

ISBN: 0-7432-4752-3

Editorial managers: *Odile Perrard & Valérie Tognali*
Proofreading: *Paul Hines-Elisabeth Ayre*
Art director: *Sabine Houplain*
Layout: *bigre !*

Photo engraving: Euresys à Baisieux
Printed in Trieste, Italy, by Editoriale Lloyd
Registration: 17028, November 2001